Acclaim for Barbara Stoler Miller's
new translation of the *Bhagavad-Gita*

"By far the best, really quite by far. . . . I will be very surprised if [this] translation will not become the one in standard use."

> —John Stratton Hawley,
> Professor of Asian Languages and Literature,
> University of Washington

"As an expression of quintessential doctrine, the *Gita* is, as it were, the Sermon on the Mount of Hinduism. . . . Professor Miller's poetic translation presents the teachings of the *Gita* to us in lucid language and strong, rhythmic verse. It is a translation that affords pleasure no less than edification."

> —Dr. Robert F. Goheen,
> former Ambassador to India
> and past President of Princeton University

"I believe that Miller's is the translation for her generation. . . . It is astonishing how she has expressed in the idiom of our own time ideas that are central to the text in a fashion that I am convinced illuminates the original meaning."

> —Ainslee Embree,
> Professor of History, Columbia University

the bhaga

KRISHNA'S COUNSEL IN TIME OF WAR

A TRANSLATION BY BARBARA STOLER MILLER

BANTAM BOOKS

TORONTO · NEW YORK · LONDON · SYDNEY · AUCKLAND

For Gwenn

**for her sense
of the ways we are**

THE BHAGAVAD-GITA

A Bantam Classic edition / August 1986

ISBN 0-553-21210-9

Published simultaneously in the United States and Canada

Bantam Books are published by Bantam Books, Inc. Its trademark, consisting of the words "Bantam Books" and the portrayal of a rooster, is Registered in U.S. Patent and Trademark Office and in other countries. Marca Registrada. Bantam Books, Inc., 666 Fifth Avenue, New York, New York 10103.

CONTENTS

INTRODUCTION

The Bhagavad-Gita: *Context and Text*

The *Bhagavad-Gita* has been the exemplary text of Hindu
culture for centuries, both in India and in the West. The
Sanskrit title *Bhagavad-Gita* has usually been interpreted
to mean "Song of the Lord," but this is misleading. It is
not a lyric but a philosophical poem, composed in the
form of a dialogue between the warrior Arjuna and his
charioteer, the god Krishna.

As we read the *Bhagavad-Gita* today we can understand the paralyzing conflict Arjuna suffers knowing that
the enemies it is his warrior duty to destroy are his own
kinsmen and teachers. We can sympathize with his im-
pulse to shrink from the violence he sees in the human
condition, and we can learn from the ways Krishna
teaches him to understand his own and others' mortality.
Krishna's exposition of the relationship between death,
sacrifice, and devotion dramatizes the Hindu idea that
one must heroically confront death in order to transcend
the limits of worldly existence. We may not share Arjuna's developing faith in Krishna's authority or be convinced by Krishna's insistence that one must perform
one's sacred duty, even when it requires violence. But if
we listen carefully to the compelling arguments and imagery of the discourse, we cannot but hear the voice of a
larger reality.

The dramatic moral crisis that is central to the
Bhagavad-Gita has inspired centuries of Indian philosophers and practical men of wisdom, as well as Western
thinkers such as Thoreau, Emerson, and Eliot. Interpretations of the *Gita*, as it is commonly referred to in India,

are as varied as the figures who have commented on it. From Shankara, the great Hindu philosopher of the eighth century, to Mahatma Gandhi, the leader of India's independence struggle in the twentieth century, each thinker has emphasized the path to spiritual liberation that was suited to his view of reality. These various interpretations reflect the intentionally multifaceted message of Krishna's teaching. The *Gita*'s significance for Hindu life continues to be debated in India today.

Hinduism is not based on the teachings of a founder, such as Buddha, Christ, or Muhammad. It has evolved over centuries through the continual interplay of diverse religious beliefs and practices: popular local cults; orthodox traditions, including the ancient Vedic hymns, the ritual texts of the Brahmanas, and the mystical Upanishads; as well as heterodox challenges from Buddhist and Jain ideas and institutions. Even the word *Hindu* is a foreign idea, used by Arab invaders in the eighth century A.D. to refer to the customs and beliefs of people who worshipped sectarian gods such as Vishnu and Shiva.

Although the *Gita* exists as an independent sacred text, its placement within the sixth book of the great Indian war epic, the *Mahabharata*, gives it a concrete context. The religious and cultural life of the Indian subcontinent, and much of the rest of Asia, has been deeply influenced by the *Mahabharata*, as well as by the *Ramayana*, the other ancient Indian epic. Both poems have their roots in legendary events that took place in the period following the entry of nomadic Indo-Aryan–speaking tribes into northwestern India around 1200 B.C. The composition of the epics began as these tribes settled in the river valleys of the Indus and the Ganges during the first millennium B.C., when their nomadic sacrificial cults began to develop into what are now the religious traditions of Hinduism.

The Hindu concept of religion is expressed by the Sanskrit term *dharma* ("sacred duty"), which refers to the moral order that sustains the cosmos, society, and the individual. The continual reinterpretation of *dharma* attests to its significance in Indian civilization. Derived from a

Sanskrit form meaning "that which sustains," within Hindu culture it generally means religiously ordained duty, that is, the code of conduct appropriate to each group in the hierarchically ordered Hindu society. Theoretically, right and wrong are not absolute in this system; practically, right and wrong are decided according to the categories of social rank, kinship, and stage of life. For modern Westerners who have been raised on ideals of universality and egalitarianism, this relativity of values and obligations is the aspect of Hinduism most difficult to understand. However, without an attempt to understand it, the Hindu view of life remains opaque.

The epics are repositories of myths, ideals, and concepts that Hindu culture has always drawn upon to represent aspects of *dharma*. As befits their social position as warrior-kings, the figures of the epic heroes embody order and sacred duty *(dharma);* while their foes, whether human or demonic, embody chaos *(adharma)*. The rituals of warrior life and the demands of sacred duty define the religious and moral meaning of heroism throughout the *Mahabharata*. Acts of heroism are characterized less by physical prowess than by the fulfillment of *dharma,* which often involves extraordinary forms of sacrifice, penance, devotion to a divine authority, and spiritual victory over evil. The distinctive martial religion of this epic emerges from a synthesis of values derived from the ritual traditions of the Vedic sacrificial cult combined with loyalty to a personal deity.

Most scholars agree that the *Mahabharata* was composed over the centuries between 400 B.C. and A.D. 400. Beyond its kernel story of internecine war, it is difficult to summarize. The work has its stylistic and mythological roots in the *Rig Veda;* its narrative sources are the oral tales of a tribal war fought in the Punjab early in the first millennium B.C. As the tradition was taken over by professional storytellers and intellectuals, many sorts of legend, myth, and speculative thought were absorbed, including the *Bhagavad-Gita,* which belongs to that layer of the epic which took form around the first century A.D. In its present form the *Mahabharata* is a rich encyclopedia of ancient Indian culture consisting of over one hundred thousand verses divided into eighteen books. The multiple layers of the text reflect its long history as well as attempts to reconcile conflicting religious and social values.

The epic's main narrative revolves around a feud over succession to the ancient kingdom of Kurukshetra in northern India. The rivals are two sets of cousins descended from the legendary king Bharata—the five sons of Pandu and the one hundred sons of Dhritarashtra. The feud itself is based on genealogical complications that are a result of a series of divine interventions. Pandu had become king because his elder brother, Dhritarashtra, was congenitally blind and thus ineligible for direct succession to the throne. But Pandu was unable to beget offspring because of a curse that forbade him intercourse with his two wives on penalty of death. After a long reign he renounces the throne and retires to the forest, where he fathers five sons (the Pandava brothers) with the help of five gods, and then dies.

The Pandava brothers are taken to be educated with their cousins at the court of Dhritarashtra, who has assumed the throne as regent in the absence of another adult heir. The princes' two teachers are their great-uncle Bhishma, who is revered for the spiritual power symbolized by his vow of celibacy, and the priest Drona, who is a master of archery and the teacher chosen by Bhishma to educate the princes in the martial arts. Arjuna becomes Drona's favored pupil when he vows to avenge his teacher's honor at the end of his training. The Pandavas excel their cousins in every warrior skill and virtue, which arouses the jealousy of Dhritarashtra's eldest son, Duryodhana.

Although Yudhishthira, Pandu's eldest son, has the legitimate right to be king, Duryodhana covets the throne, and in various episodes he attempts to assassinate his cousins or otherwise frustrate their rights. After thirteen years of exile imposed on them as the penalty for Yudhishthira's defeat in a crooked dice game played as part of a ritual, the Pandavas return to reclaim their kingdom. Duryodhana's refusal to step aside makes war inevitable. The description of the eighteen-day-long battle and concomitant philosophizing by various teachers takes up the bulk of the epic. The battle ends with the triumph of the Pandavas over their cousins—the triumph of order over chaos.

The setting of the *Gita* is the battlefield of Kurukshetra as the war is about to begin. It is not only a physical place but is representative of a state of mind. When the assembled troops are arrayed on the field awaiting battle, the sage Vyasa, the traditional author of the *Mahabharata*, appears to the blind Dhritarashtra and grants him a boon. He will be able to hear an account of the battle from Sanjaya, who is endowed with immediate vision of all things past, present, and future, thus enabling him to see every detail of the battle. Vyasa says to Dhritarashtra: "Sanjaya shall see all the events of the battle directly. He shall have a divine inner eye. . . . O King, Sanjaya has an inner eye. He will tell you everything about the battle. He will be all-knowing. Whenever he thinks with his mind, Sanjaya will see everything taking place during day or night, in public or in secret."

Sanjaya, the visionary narrator who serves as the personal bard and charioteer of Dhritarashtra, is thus the mediating voice through whom the audience of the *Gita* learns Krishna's secret teaching. Through Sanjaya's retelling, the mystery of life and death revealed to Arjuna enters into the bardic tradition that preserves it for all to hear. Sanjaya's role in the *Gita* begins with the opening verse, spoken by Dhritarashtra.

Sanjaya, tell me what my sons
and the sons of Pandu did when they met,
wanting to battle on the field of Kuru,
on the field of sacred duty?

This question reverberates through the entire text, equating the field of internecine war with the field of sacred duty, where Arjuna's personal moral struggle is fought. In answer to Dhritarashtra's question, Sanjaya starts his recitation by recounting the dialogue about the war that he overhears between Duryodhana and Drona. This functions like a dramatic prologue, setting the scene of the *Gita* and preparing the audience to listen to Arjuna's dialogue with Krishna.

When Krishna and Arjuna enter Sanjaya's narrative, the focus shifts from action on the field of war to Arjuna's inner conflict. Arjuna's dejection is the spiritual abyss into which Krishna's teaching pours. In his misery Arjuna rejects the conventional rewards of battle and is filled with pity in face of the horrors of war. The dialogue that follows is aesthetically grounded in the tension between Arjuna's state of pity and his basic heroism. The representation of Arjuna's involuntary physical responses, such as his trembling body and bristling hair, dramatizes the pity he feels before the specter of disorder and impending slaughter. In Hindu aesthetic theory such responses are considered highly significant because they arise from inner feeling and cannot be simulated.

> Standing on their great chariot
> yoked with white stallions,
> Krishna and Arjuna, Pandu's son,
> sounded their divine conches.
> . . . .
>
> Arjuna, his war flag a rampant monkey,
> saw Dhritarashtra's sons assembled
> as weapons were ready to clash,
> and he lifted his bow.
>
> He told his charioteer:
> "Krishna,
> halt my chariot
> between the armies!"
> . . . .
>
> He surveyed his elders
> and companions in both armies,
> all his kinsmen
> assembled together.

Dejected, filled with strange pity,
he said this:
"Krishna, I see my kinsmen
gathered here, wanting war.

My limbs sink,
my mouth is parched,
my body trembles,
the hair bristles on my flesh.

The magic bow slips
from my hand, my skin burns,
I cannot stand still,
my mind reels.

I see omens of chaos,
Krishna; I see no good
in killing my kinsmen
in battle."

For Arjuna, and for the audience of the *Gita*, Krishna
is a companion and teacher, as well as the god who com-
mands devotion. Krishna's mythology suggests that he is
a tribal hero transformed into cult divinity. In the *Gita*,
Krishna is the incarnation of cosmic power, who periodi-
cally descends to earth to accomplish the restoration of
order in times of chaos. The mundane and cosmic levels
of his activity are interwoven to provide the background
for his role as divine charioteer to Arjuna. The mightiest
warrior in the epic, Arjuna is characterized not only by
his physical prowess but by his spiritual prowess, which
involves a mystical friendship with Krishna. From the
start Arjuna knows that his charioteer is no ordinary
mortal; he begs Krishna to dispel his uncertainty, and
Krishna speaks with the authority of omniscience. As Arjuna's confidence and faith increase, the power of
Krishna's divinity gradually unfolds before him in all its
terrible glory, and Arjuna comes to see himself mirrored
in the divine. Krishna's revelation of the cosmic spectacle
forces Arjuna to accept the necessity of his own part in it.
Krishna directly addresses Arjuna's emotional at-

tachments, uncertainty, and inability to act, and in the process, he enlarges Arjuna's awareness beyond the personal and social values that Arjuna holds sacred, compelling him to recognize why he must fight. Krishna insists that Arjuna's pity is really weakness and that the practice of true duty does not arise from personal passion but is part of a larger order that demands detachment. According to Krishna, Arjuna's objections to killing his relatives are based on the same subjective, worldly desire that blinds his foes to their folly. Krishna's solution lies on another level, one where oppositions coexist within his cosmic knowledge. Krishna, the omnipotent lord, teaches that the warrior's ordained duty (dharma) is grounded in the reciprocal relationship between cosmic and human action (karma), which is crucial to universal order.

In order to explore the paradoxical interconnectedness of disciplined action and freedom, Krishna develops his ideas in improvisational ways, not in linear arguments that lead to immediate resolution. The dialogue moves through a series of questions and answers that elucidate key words, concepts, and seeming contradictions in order to establish the crucial relationships among duty (dharma), discipline (yoga), action (karma), knowledge (jñāna), and devotion (bhakti). The concepts are drawn from many sources. Most important are several ancient systems of thought: Sankhya, the dualistic philosophy that analyzes the constituents of phenomenal existence; Yoga, the code of practical discipline based on dualism; Vedanta, the pantheistic doctrine of metaphysical knowledge; as well as Buddhism. Krishna teaches Arjuna the way to resolve the dilemma of renunciation and action. Freedom lies, not in the renunciation of the world, but in disciplined action (karmayoga). Put concretely, all action is to be both performed without attachment to the fruit of action (karmaphalāsaṅga) and dedicated with loving devotion to Krishna. Disciplined action within the context of devotion is essential to the religious life envisioned in the Gita.

Each of the eighteen teachings that comprise the Gita highlights some aspect of Krishna's doctrine, but there is much repetition throughout them as the central themes are developed and subtly interpreted within the text. The text also has a broader triadic structure. In the first six teachings the dramatic narrative modulates into a series of theoretical and practical teachings on self-knowledge and the nature of action. The third and fourth teachings develop the crucial relation between sacrifice and action. The fifth and sixth teachings explore the tension between renunciation and action; Arjuna's query is resolved in the ideal of disciplined action. It is Arjuna's probing questions and his dissatisfaction with the apparent inconsistencies in Krishna's answers that expose Arjuna's state of mind and open him now to more advanced teachings. In the seventh teaching, focus shifts toward knowledge of Krishna. The language of paradox intensifies and hyperbole heightens, culminating in the dazzling theophany of the eleventh teaching. The theophany ends in a cadence on devotion, and the twelfth teaching develops this idea. Arjuna is transformed, not by a systematic argument, but by a mystical teaching in which Krishna becomes the object of Arjuna's intense devotion (bhakti). The representation of Arjuna's mystical experience of Krishna is poetically structured within the dialogue form to engage the participation of the audience in its drama.

In the final six teachings, the dialogue recedes as Krishna emphatically recapitulates the basic ideas he has already taught and integrates them into the doctrine of devotion. Devotion allows for a resolution of the conflict between the worldly life of allotted duties and the life of renunciation. By purging his mind of attachments and dedicating the fruits of his actions to Krishna, Arjuna can continue to act in a world of pain without suffering despair. The core of this devotion to Krishna is discipline (yoga), which enables the warrior to control his passions and become a man of discipline (yogī).

Arjuna can dedicate himself to Krishna only after his delusions about the nature of life and death have been dispelled and he has the power to see Krishna in his cosmic form. Once he has been instructed by Krishna in the most profound mysteries, Arjuna asks to see Krishna's immutable self. In the eleventh teaching, Krishna gives him a divine eye with which to see the majesty of his cosmic order. The aspect of himself that Krishna reveals to Arjuna on the battlefield embodies time's deadly destructiveness: a fearsome explosion of countless eyes, bellies, mouths, ornaments, and weapons—gleaming like the fiery sun that illumines the world.

At this juncture Sanjaya reenters the drama, interrupting the dialogue he is recounting and speaking in his own voice, as the bard who shares with the blind king and the audience what was revealed to Arjuna:

> If the light of a thousand suns
> were to rise in the sky at once,
> it would be like the light
> of that great spirit.
>
> Arjuna saw all the universe
> in its many ways and parts
> standing as one in the body
> of the god of gods.
>
> Then filled with amazement,
> his hair bristling on his flesh,
> Arjuna bowed his head to the god,
> joined his hands in homage, and spoke.

Sanjaya speaks twice again within this teaching, each time intensifying the theophany for his audience. Then the text continues in Arjuna's stammering voice of terror:

> Seeing the many mouths
> and eyes
> of your great form,
> its many arms,
> thighs, feet,
> bellies, and fangs,
> the worlds tremble
> and so do I.
> . . . .

Seeing the fangs
protruding
from your mouths
like the fires of time,
I lose my bearings
and I find no refuge;
be gracious, Lord of Gods,
Shelter of the Universe.

Arjuna begs, "Tell me—who are you in this terrible
form?" Krishna responds:

I am time grown old,
creating world destruction
set in motion
to annihilate the worlds;
even without you,
all these warriors
arrayed in hostile ranks
will cease to exist.

Therefore, arise
and win glory!
Conquer your foes
and fulfill your kingship!
They are already
slain by me.
Be just my instrument,
the archer at my side!

Here the divine charioteer reveals his terrifying identity as creator and destroyer of everything in the universe. As destroyer, he has already destroyed both
mighty armies. As creator, his cosmic purpose is to keep
order in the universe, as well as in the human world. Although the sight of Krishna's horrific power is too much
for Arjuna to bear and he begs to see him again in his
calmer aspect, the experience brings Arjuna to the realization that his duty to fight is intimately linked to
Krishna's divine activity. Overwhelmed by the vision of

time's inexorable violence embodied in his charioteer, Arjuna sees the inevitability of his actions. He realizes that by performing his warrior duty with absolute devotion to Krishna, he can unite with Krishna's cosmic purpose and free himself from the crippling attachments that bind mortals to eternal suffering.

In the thirteenth teaching Krishna redefines the battlefield as the human body, the material realm in which one struggles to know oneself. It is less a physical place than a symbolic field of interior warfare, a place of clashing forces, all of which have their origin in Krishna's ultimate reality. In the teachings that follow, various aspects of Krishna's material nature *(prakṛti)* are analyzed in terms of the three fundamental qualities *(guṇa)* that constitute it—lucidity *(sattva)*, passion *(rajas)*, and dark inertia *(tamas)*. The scheme of natural qualities, introduced in the third teaching, is now elaborated to amplify Krishna's relation to the world from the perspectives of metaphysics, morality, and religious tradition. In the long final teaching, in response to Arjuna's request to know the distinction between renunciation *(sannyāsa)* and relinquishment *(tyāga)* of action, Krishna returns to the central dilemma of action. He reiterates the crucial connection between action and devotion, and the dialogue closes with Arjuna's avowal that his delusion is destroyed and he is ready to act on Krishna's words.

At every stage of Arjuna's dramatic journey of self-discovery, the charioteer Krishna is aware of his pupil's spiritual conflict and guides him to the appropriate path for resolving it. Krishna urges him not to resign himself to killing but instead to renounce his selfish attachment to the fruits of his actions. By learning how to discipline his emotion and his action, Arjuna journeys far without ever leaving the battlefield. Krishna draws him into a universe beyond the world of everyday experience but keeps forcing him back to wage the battle of life. He advocates, on the one hand, the life of action and moral duty, and on the other, the transcendence of empirical experience in search of knowledge and liberation. Though much of Krishna's teaching seems remote from the moral chaos that Arjuna envisions will be a consequence of his killing his kinsmen, Krishna's doctrine of disciplined action is a way of bringing order to life's destructive aspect. When the puzzled Arjuna asks, "Why do you urge me to do this act of violence?" Krishna does not condone physical violence. Instead, he identifies the real enemy as desire, due to attachment, an enemy that can only be overcome by arming oneself with discipline and acting to transcend the narrow limits of individual desire.

The text of the *Gita* ends by commenting on itself through the witness of Sanjaya, who re-creates the dialogue in all its compelling power as he keeps remembering it. He recalls for the blind king Dhritarashtra, and for every other member of his audience, the correspondence between Krishna's wondrous form and the language of poetry that represents that form. Anyone who listens to his words gains consciousness of Krishna's presence. Sanjaya says:

As I heard this wondrous dialogue
between Krishna and Arjuna,
the man of great soul,
the hair bristled on my flesh.

By grace of the epic poet Vyasa, I heard
the secret of supreme discipline
recounted by Krishna himself,
lord of discipline incarnate.

O King, when I keep remembering
this wondrous and holy dialogue
between Krishna and Arjuna,
I rejoice again and again.

In my memory I recall again
and again Krishna's wondrous form—
great is my amazement, King;
I rejoice again and again.

TRANSLATOR'S NOTE

The decision to attempt this translation of the *Bhagavad-Gita* was not taken lightly. The *Gita*'s dramatic power, compressed language, and network of complex ideas offer a daunting challenge to the translator. I have often thought of T. S. Eliot's comparison of its greatness as a philosophical poem to that of the *Divine Comedy,* and this colored my response when Allen Mandelbaum, as one of Dante's translators, proposed that I undertake a new translation of the *Gita.*

The *Gita* has been translated into English and other Western languages in many varied forms since the first English version was published by Charles Wilkins in 1785. The reception of the *Gita* reflects Western responses to the broader Indian culture. Westerners have been discovering India since antiquity, when members of Alexander the Great's expedition to India, in the fourth century B.C., recorded their impressions in terms of fabulous exoticism. A tradition of myths and fables about India continued to appear in the travel accounts of Greek and Latin authors and centuries afterward in the writings of Arab historians and Portuguese missionaries. Not until the last half of the eighteenth century were there serious attempts to study Indian literature. Sir William Jones, a judge of the supreme court in Calcutta and an erudite linguist of the time, recognized the relationship of European languages to Persian and Sanskrit, rejecting the prevalent view that all languages were derived from Hebrew, which had supposedly been garbled in the Tower of Babel. With his friend Charles Wilkins, a merchant in the service of the East India Company in Bengal, Jones produced the first direct translations of Sanskrit works into English. The *Bhagavad-Gita* was followed by Wilkins's translation of the *Hitopadesa* (1787), Jones's *Sakuntala* (1789), the *Gitagovinda* (1792), and the *Institutes of Hindoo Law* (1794). As these translations circulated in Europe and America they formed the basis of modern Western conceptions of ancient Indian culture. Despite a growing sympathy for Indian literature on the part of the German writers Schlegel, Humboldt, and Goethe, and Emerson and Thoreau in America, Western reaction to these works was generally negative.

James Mill, in *A History of British India*, published in 1817, argued that even when an Indian text might appear sensible, it inevitably contained some "monstrous exhibition," such as Krishna's theophany in the *Gita*. Thomas Babington Macaulay in his "Minute on Education," written in 1835 to justify the decision that all higher education in British India supported by government funds be conducted in the English language and follow the curriculum prevalent in English schools, epitomized the dominant colonial attitude of his time:

> I have no knowledge of either Sanscrit or Arabic. But I have done what I could to form a correct estimate of their value. I have read translations of the most celebrated Arabic and Sanscrit works. I have conversed both here and at home with men distinguished by their proficiency in the Eastern tongues. I am quite ready to take the Oriental learning at the valuation of the Orientalists themselves. I have never found one among them who could deny that a single shelf of a good European library was worth the whole native literature of India and Arabia.

When encountering the literature of a foreign culture, especially one as complex as that of India, our tendency is to make generalizations. A more accurate appreciation requires careful reading on our part, as well as the use of our sympathetic imagination. The translation at hand is an attempt to engage the close attention and sympathy of contemporary readers who have no prior technical knowledge of Indian thought. When I first read the *Gita*, almost thirty years ago, in the translation by Swami Prabhavananda and Christopher Isherwood, I was deeply impressed by the power of its dovetailing images of external war and internal human struggle. That translation, published in 1944, still has merit for the uninitiated reader, but as I have studied the *Gita* in its original Sanskrit and read it with students over the years, I have felt that the space between Sanskrit and English could be bridged more directly, without sacrificing the work's philosophical subtlety or poetic energy. The *Gita* has drama, monumentality, and strong narrative movement; I have attempted to reproduce these in the translation to give the reader easier access to the meaning of the original text. This dimension of the *Gita* is usually ignored by scholars, who puzzle over the elliptical philosophical discourse without realizing that much of its meaning lies in its expressive structures. To reflect its rhetorical rhythms I have also preserved the metrical variations in the original text. The prevailing epic narrative stanza is a quatrain with eight syllables to each quarter (*śloka*); I have translated it into a four-line stanza of free verse. The more complicated epic meter, with eleven syllables to each quarter (*triṣṭubh*), appears at moments of greater intensity in the text; I have rendered it by a more elaborate stanza of eight lines.

My introduction to the context and the text, and the lexicon of key words are intended to amplify the translation. Although in many cases no single English term exactly expresses the Sanskrit term, and a case may be made for using alternative translations in different contexts, I have chosen to maintain a consistency of technical terms in translation in order to represent the texture of the original. Almost every Sanskrit term has been given the same English translation each time it occurs. The lexicon of the key English words I have used was consciously created as an alternative to notes on individual words and concepts. Such a lexicon should help the English reader to grasp the central concepts of the text. The numerous epithets of Krishna and Arjuna, such as *Madhusudana*, "Slayer of Demon Madhu" for Krishna, or *Kaunteya*, "Son of Kunti" for Arjuna, have not been translated. Their meanings have resonance for an Indian audience, but for other readers they have little significance and are cumbersome in translation, so they have generally been normalized to the names Krishna and Arjuna. In certain places, especially in the opening narrative verses and in the section preceding the theophany, I have expanded the translation of proper names into English epithets that clarify the context.

The afterword on Thoreau's response to the *Gita* is meant to lead the reader out of the ancient Indian epic world and offer a more familiar interpretive perspective on the central issues of Krishna's discourse. In this process the text itself becomes a way of reflecting on what is close at hand.

I have been helped in my work by a few people in many ways. Without Stanley Insler's insistence that the text deserved a clearer and stronger voice in English, I would not have begun. LuAnn Walther encouraged me from that start by her interest in the project. Barry Moser, in our discussions of the *Gita*'s central imagery, has heightened my awareness of the visual music inside the poem. My friends have at various stages shared their wisdom with me. Helen Bacon, Susan Bergholz, Srivatsa Goswami, Orrin Hein, Linda Hess, Hidei Ishiguro, Stella Kramrisch, Dorothy Norman, Karl Potter, A. K. Ramanujan, Ravi Ravindra, and Brian Smith have all helped me in some special way. Once the first draft of the translation was completed, I read the Sanskrit text anew with my students Peter Banos, Nadine Berardi, Barbara Gombach, Eric Huberman, Michaelangelo Allocca, and Francis Tiso. They know how much I learned from their probing questions and spirited criticism of my interpretations. To a great extent this translation is theirs too.

This is the use of memory:
For liberation—not less of love but expanding
Of love beyond desire, and so liberation
From the future as well as the past.

—T. S. Eliot,
"Little Gidding" III,
The Four Quartets

the bhagavad-gita

KRISHNA'S COUNSEL
IN TIME OF WAR

The First Teaching

ARJUNA'S DEJECTION

Dhritarashtra

Sanjaya, tell me what my sons
and the sons of Pandu did when they met,
wanting to battle on the field of Kuru,
on the field of sacred duty? 1

Sanjaya

Your son Duryodhana, the king,
seeing the Pandava forces arrayed,
approached his teacher Drona
and spoke in command. 2

"My teacher, see
the great Pandava army arrayed
by Drupada's son,
your pupil, intent on revenge. 3

Here are heroes, mighty archers
equal to Bhima and Arjuna in warfare,
Yuyudhana, Virata, and Drupada,
your sworn foe on his great chariot. 4

Here too are Dhrishtaketu, Cekitana,
and the brave king of Benares;
Purujit, Kuntibhoja,
and the manly king of the Shibis. 5

Yudhamanyu is bold,
and Uttamaujas is brave;
the sons of Subhadra and Draupadi
all command great chariots.   6

Now, honored priest, mark
the superb men on our side
as I tell you the names
of my army's leaders.   7

They are you and Bhishma,
Karna and Kripa, a victor in battles,
your own son Ashvatthama,
Vikarna, and the son of Somadatta.   8

Many other heroes also risk
their lives for my sake,
bearing varied weapons
and skilled in the ways of war.   9

Guarded by Bhishma, the strength
of our army is without limit;
but the strength of their army,
guarded by Bhima, is limited.   10

In all the movements of battle,
you and your men,
stationed according to plan,
must guard Bhishma well!"   11

Bhishma, fiery elder of the Kurus,
roared his lion's roar
and blew his conch horn,
exciting Duryodhana's delight.   12

Conches and kettledrums,
cymbals, tabors, and trumpets
were sounded at once
and the din of tumult arose.   13

Standing on their great chariot
yoked with white stallions,
Krishna and Arjuna, Pandu's son,
sounded their divine conches.   14

Krishna blew Pancajanya, won from a demon;
Arjuna blew Devadatta, a gift of the gods;
fierce wolf-bellied Bhima blew Paundra,
his great conch of the east.   15

Yudhishthira, Kunti's son, the king,
blew Anantavijaya, conch of boundless victory;
his twin brothers Nakula and Sahadeva
blew conches resonant and jewel toned.   16

The king of Benares, a superb archer,
and Shikhandin on his great chariot,
Drishtadyumna, Virata, and indomitable Satyaki,
all blew their conches.   17

Drupada, with his five grandsons,
and Subhadra's strong-armed son,
each in his turn blew
their conches, O King.   18

The noise tore the hearts
of Dhritarashtra's sons,
and tumult echoed
through heaven and earth.   19

Arjuna, his war flag a rampant monkey,
saw Dhritarashtra's sons assembled
as weapons were ready to clash,
and he lifted his bow.   20

He told his charioteer:
    "Krishna,
    halt my chariot
    between the armies!   21

Far enough for me to see
these men who lust for war,
ready to fight with me
in the strain of battle.   22

I see men gathered here,
eager to fight,
bent on serving the folly
of Dhritarashtra's son."   23

When Arjuna had spoken,
Krishna halted
their splendid chariot
between the armies.   24

Facing Bhishma and Drona
and all the great kings,
he said, "Arjuna, see
the Kuru men assembled here!"   25

Arjuna saw them standing there:
fathers, grandfathers, teachers,
uncles, brothers, sons,
grandsons, and friends.   26

He surveyed his elders
and companions in both armies,
all his kinsmen
assembled together.   27

Dejected, filled with strange pity,
he said this:
     "Krishna, I see my kinsmen
     gathered here, wanting war.   28

     My limbs sink,
     my mouth is parched,
     my body trembles,
     the hair bristles on my flesh.   29

The magic bow slips
from my hand, my skin burns,
I cannot stand still,
my mind reels.   30

I see omens of chaos,
Krishna; I see no good
in killing my kinsmen
in battle.   31

Krishna, I seek no victory,
or kingship or pleasures.
What use to us are kingship,
delights, or life itself?   32

We sought kingship, delights,
and pleasures for the sake of those
assembled to abandon their lives
and fortunes in battle.   33

They are teachers, fathers, sons,
and grandfathers, uncles, grandsons,
fathers and brothers of wives,
and other men of our family.   34

I do not want to kill them
even if I am killed, Krishna;
not for kingship of all three worlds,
much less for the earth!   35

What joy is there for us, Krishna,
in killing Dhritarashtra's sons?
Evil will haunt us if we kill them,
though their bows are drawn to kill.   36

Honor forbids us to kill
our cousins, Dhritarashtra's sons;
how can we know happiness
if we kill our own kinsmen?   37

The greed that distorts their reason
blinds them to the sin they commit
in ruining the family, blinds them
to the crime of betraying friends.   38

How can we ignore the wisdom
of turning from this evil
when we see the sin
of family destruction, Krishna?   39

When the family is ruined,
the timeless laws of family duty
perish; and when duty is lost,
chaos overwhelms the family.   40

In overwhelming chaos, Krishna,
women of the family are corrupted;
and when women are corrupted,
disorder is born in society.   41

This discord drags the violators
and the family itself to hell;
for ancestors fall when rites
of offering rice and water lapse.   42

The sins of men who violate
the family create disorder in society
that undermines the constant laws
of caste and family duty.   43

Krishna, we have heard
that a place in hell
is reserved for men
who undermine family duties.   44

I lament the great sin
we commit when our greed
for kingship and pleasures
drives us to kill our kinsmen.   45

If Dhritarashtra's armed sons
kill me in battle when I am unarmed
and offer no resistance,
it will be my reward."   46

Saying this in the time of war,
Arjuna slumped into the chariot
and laid down his bow and arrows,
his mind tormented by grief.   47

The Second Teaching

PHILOSOPHY AND
SPIRITUAL DISCIPLINE

Sanjaya

Arjuna sat dejected,
filled with pity,
his sad eyes blurred by tears.
Krishna gave him counsel.   1

Lord Krishna

Why this cowardice
in time of crisis, Arjuna?
The coward is ignoble, shameful,
foreign to the ways of heaven.   2

Don't yield to impotence!
It is unnatural in you!
Banish this petty weakness from your heart.
Rise to the fight, Arjuna!   3

Arjuna

Krishna, how can I fight
against Bhishma and Drona
with arrows
when they deserve my worship?   4

It is better in this world
to beg for scraps of food
than to eat meals
smeared with the blood
of elders I killed
at the height of their power
while their goals
were still desires.   5

We don't know which weight
is worse to bear—
our conquering them
or their conquering us.
We will not want to live
if we kill
the sons of Dhritarashtra
assembled before us.   6

The flaw of pity
blights my very being;
conflicting sacred duties
confound my reason.
I ask you to tell me
decisively—Which is better?
I am your pupil.
Teach me what I seek!   7

I see nothing
that could drive away
the grief
that withers my senses;
even if I won kingdoms
of unrivaled wealth
on earth
and sovereignty over gods.   8

Sanjaya

Arjuna told this
to Krishna—then saying,
"I shall not fight,"
he fell silent.   9

Mocking him gently,
Krishna gave this counsel
as Arjuna sat dejected,
between the two armies.   10

Lord Krishna

You grieve for those beyond grief,
and you speak words of insight;
but learned men do not grieve
for the dead or the living.   11

Never have I not existed,
nor you, nor these kings;
and never in the future
shall we cease to exist.   12

Just as the embodied self
enters childhood, youth, and old age,
so does it enter another body;
this does not confound a steadfast man.   13

Contacts with matter make us feel
heat and cold, pleasure and pain.
Arjuna, you must learn to endure
fleeting things—they come and go!   14

When these cannot torment a man,
when suffering and joy are equal
for him and he has courage,
he is fit for immortality.   15

Nothing of nonbeing comes to be,
nor does being cease to exist;
the boundary between these two
is seen by men who see reality.   16

Indestructible is the presence
that pervades all this;
no one can destroy
this unchanging reality.   17

Our bodies are known to end,
but the embodied self is enduring,
indestructible, and immeasurable;
therefore, Arjuna, fight the battle!   18

He who thinks this self a killer
and he who thinks it killed,
both fail to understand;
it does not kill, nor is it killed.   19

It is not born,
it does not die;
having been,
it will never not be;
unborn, enduring,
constant, and primordial,
it is not killed
when the body is killed.   20

Arjuna, when a man knows the self
to be indestructible, enduring, unborn,
unchanging, how does he kill
or cause anyone to kill?   21

As a man discards
worn-out clothes
to put on new
and different ones,
so the embodied self
discards
its worn-out bodies
to take on other new ones.   22

Weapons do not cut it,
fire does not burn it,
waters do not wet it,
wind does not wither it.   23

It cannot be cut or burned;
it cannot be wet or withered;
it is enduring, all-pervasive,
fixed, immovable, and timeless.   24

It is called unmanifest,
inconceivable, and immutable;
since you know that to be so,
you should not grieve!   25

If you think of its birth
and death as ever-recurring,
then too, Great Warrior,
you have no cause to grieve!   26

Death is certain for anyone born,
and birth is certain for the dead;
since the cycle is inevitable,
you have no cause to grieve!   27

Creatures are unmanifest in origin,
manifest in the midst of life,
and unmanifest again in the end.
Since this is so, why do you lament?   28

Rarely someone
sees it,
rarely another
speaks it,
rarely anyone
hears it—
even hearing it,
no one really knows it.   29

The self embodied in the body
of every being is indestructible;
you have no cause to grieve
for all these creatures, Arjuna!   30

Look to your own duty;
do not tremble before it;
nothing is better for a warrior
than a battle of sacred duty.   31

The doors of heaven open
for warriors who rejoice
to have a battle like this
thrust on them by chance.   32

If you fail to wage this war
of sacred duty,
you will abandon your own duty
and fame only to gain evil.   33

People will tell
of your undying shame,
and for a man of honor
shame is worse than death.   34

The great chariot warriors will think
you deserted in fear of battle;
you will be despised
by those who held you in esteem.   35

Your enemies will slander you,
scorning your skill
in so many unspeakable ways—
could any suffering be worse?   36

If you are killed, you win heaven;
if you triumph, you enjoy the earth;
therefore, Arjuna, stand up
and resolve to fight the battle!   37

Impartial to joy and suffering,
gain and loss, victory and defeat,
arm yourself for the battle,
lest you fall into evil.   38

Understanding is defined in terms of philosophy;
now hear it in spiritual discipline.
Armed with this understanding, Arjuna,
you will escape the bondage of action.   39

No effort in this world
is lost or wasted;
a fragment of sacred duty
saves you from great fear.   40

This understanding is unique
in its inner core of resolve;
diffuse and pointless are the ways
irresolute men understand.   41

Undiscerning men who delight
in the tenets of ritual lore
utter florid speech, proclaiming,
"There is nothing else!"   42

Driven by desire, they strive after heaven
and contrive to win powers and delights,
but their intricate ritual language
bears only the fruit of action in rebirth.   43

Obsessed with powers and delights,
their reason lost in words,
they do not find in contemplation
this understanding of inner resolve.   44

Arjuna, the realm of sacred lore
is nature—beyond its triad of qualities,
dualities, and mundane rewards,
be forever lucid, alive to your self.   45

For the discerning priest,
all of sacred lore
has no more value than a well
when water flows everywhere.   46

Be intent on action,
not on the fruits of action;
avoid attraction to the fruits
and attachment to inaction!   47

Perform actions, firm in discipline,
relinquishing attachment;
be impartial to failure and success—
this equanimity is called discipline.   48

Arjuna, action is far inferior
to the discipline of understanding;
so seek refuge in understanding—pitiful
are men drawn by fruits of action.   49

Disciplined by understanding,
one abandons both good and evil deeds;
so arm yourself for discipline—
discipline is skill in actions.   50

Wise men disciplined by understanding
relinquish the fruit born of action;
freed from these bonds of rebirth,
they reach a place beyond decay.   51

When your understanding passes beyond
the swamp of delusion,
you will be indifferent to all
that is heard in sacred lore.   52

When your understanding turns
from sacred lore to stand fixed,
immovable in contemplation,
then you will reach discipline.   53

Arjuna

Krishna, what defines a man
deep in contemplation whose insight
and thought are sure? How would he speak?
How would he sit? How would he move?   54

Lord Krishna

When he gives up desires in his mind,
is content with the self within himself,
then he is said to be a man
whose insight is sure, Arjuna.   55

When suffering does not disturb his mind,
when his craving for pleasures has vanished,
when attraction, fear, and anger are gone,
he is called a sage whose thought is sure.   56

When he shows no preference
in fortune or misfortune
and neither exults nor hates,
his insight is sure.   57

When, like a tortoise retracting
its limbs, he withdraws his senses
completely from sensuous objects,
his insight is sure.   58

Sensuous objects fade
when the embodied self abstains from food;
the taste lingers, but it too fades
in the vision of higher truth.   59

Even when a man of wisdom
tries to control them, Arjuna,
the bewildering senses
attack his mind with violence.   60

Controlling them all,
with discipline he should focus on me;
when his senses are under control,
his insight is sure.   61

Brooding about sensuous objects
makes attachment to them grow;
from attachment desire arises,
from desire anger is born.   62

From anger comes confusion;
from confusion memory lapses;
from broken memory understanding is lost;
from loss of understanding, he is ruined.   63

But a man of inner strength
whose senses experience objects
without attraction and hatred,
in self-control, finds serenity.   64

In serenity, all his sorrows
dissolve;
his reason becomes serene,
his understanding sure.   65

Without discipline,
he has no understanding or inner power;
without inner power, he has no peace;
and without peace where is joy?   66

If his mind submits to the play
of the senses,
they drive away insight,
as wind drives a ship on water.   67

So, Great Warrior, when withdrawal
of the senses
from sense objects is complete,
discernment is firm.   68

When it is night for all creatures,
a master of restraint is awake;
when they are awake, it is night
for the sage who sees reality.   69

As the mountainous depths
of the ocean
are unmoved when waters
rush into it,
so the man unmoved
when desires enter him
attains a peace that eludes
the man of many desires.   70

When he renounces all desires
and acts without craving,
possessiveness,
or individuality, he finds peace.   71

This is the place of the infinite spirit;
achieving it, one is freed from delusion;
abiding in it even at the time of death,
one finds the pure calm of infinity.   72

The Third Teaching

DISCIPLINE OF ACTION

Arjuna

If you think understanding
is more powerful than action,
why, Krishna, do you urge me
to this horrific act?   1

You confuse my understanding
with a maze of words;
speak one certain truth
so I may achieve what is good.   2

Lord Krishna

Earlier I taught the twofold
basis of good in this world—
for philosophers, disciplined knowledge;
for men of discipline, action.   3

A man cannot escape the force
of action by abstaining from actions;
he does not attain success
just by renunciation.   4

No one exists for even an instant
without performing action;
however unwilling, every being is forced
to act by the qualities of nature.   5

When his senses are controlled
but he keeps recalling
sense objects with his mind,
he is a self-deluded hypocrite.   6

When he controls his senses
with his mind and engages in the discipline
of action with his faculties of action,
detachment sets him apart.   7

Perform necessary action;
it is more powerful than inaction;
without action you even fail
to sustain your own body.   8

Action imprisons the world
unless it is done as sacrifice;
freed from attachment, Arjuna,
perform action as sacrifice!   9

When creating living beings and sacrifice,
Prajapati, the primordial creator, said:
      "By sacrifice will you procreate!
      Let it be your wish-granting cow!   10

      Foster the gods with this,
      and may they foster you;
      by enriching one another,
      you will achieve a higher good.   11

      Enriched by sacrifice, the gods
      will give you the delights you desire;
      he is a thief who enjoys their gifts
      without giving to them in return."   12

Good men eating the remnants
of sacrifice are free of any guilt,
but evil men who cook for themselves
eat the food of sin.   13

Creatures depend on food,
food comes from rain,
rain depends on sacrifice,
and sacrifice comes from action.   14

Action comes from the spirit of prayer,
whose source is OM, sound of the imperishable;
so the pervading infinite spirit
is ever present in rites of sacrifice.   15

He who fails to keep turning
the wheel here set in motion
wastes his life in sin,
addicted to the senses, Arjuna.   16

But when a man finds delight
within himself and feels inner joy
and pure contentment in himself,
there is nothing more to be done.   17

He has no stake here
in deeds done or undone,
nor does his purpose
depend on other creatures.   18

Always perform with detachment
any action you must do;
performing action with detachment,
one achieves supreme good.   19

Janaka and other ancient kings
attained perfection by action alone;
seeing the way to preserve
the world, you should act.   20

Whatever a leader does,
the ordinary people also do.
He sets the standard
for the world to follow.   21

In the three worlds,
there is nothing I must do,
nothing unattained to be attained,
yet I engage in action.   22

What if I did not engage
relentlessly in action?
Men retrace my path
at every turn, Arjuna.   23

These worlds would collapse
if I did not perform action;
I would create disorder in society,
living beings would be destroyed.   24

As the ignorant act with attachment
to actions, Arjuna,
so wise men should act with detachment
to preserve the world.   25

No wise man disturbs the understanding
of ignorant men attached to action;
he should inspire them,
performing all actions with discipline.   26

Actions are all effected
by the qualities of nature;
but deluded by individuality,
the self thinks, "I am the actor."   27

When he can discriminate
the actions of nature's qualities
and think, "The qualities depend
on other qualities," he is detached.   28

Those deluded by the qualities of nature
are attached to their actions;
a man who knows this should not upset
these dull men of partial knowledge.   29

Surrender all actions to me,
and fix your reason on your inner self;
without hope or possessiveness,
your fever subdued, fight the battle!   30

Men who always follow my thought,
trusting it without finding fault,
are freed
even by their actions.   31

But those who find fault
and fail to follow my thought,
know that they are lost fools,
deluded by every bit of knowledge.   32

Even a man of knowledge
behaves in accord with his own nature;
creatures all conform to nature;
what can one do to restrain them?   33

Attraction and hatred are poised
in the object of every sense experience;
a man must not fall prey
to these two brigands lurking on his path!   34

Your own duty done imperfectly
is better than another man's done well.
It is better to die in one's own duty;
another man's duty is perilous.   35

Arjuna

Krishna, what makes a person
commit evil
against his own will,
as if compelled by force?   36

Lord Krishna

It is desire and anger, arising
from nature's quality of passion;
know it here as the enemy,
voracious and very evil!   37

As fire is obscured by smoke
and a mirror by dirt,
as an embryo is veiled by its caul,
so is knowledge obscured by this.   38

Knowledge is obscured
by the wise man's eternal enemy,
which takes form as desire,
an insatiable fire, Arjuna.   39

The senses, mind, and understanding
are said to harbor desire;
with these desire obscures knowledge
and confounds the embodied self.   40

Therefore, first restrain
your senses, Arjuna,
then kill this evil
that ruins knowledge and judgment.   41

Men say that the senses are superior
to their objects, the mind superior to the senses,
understanding superior to the mind;
higher than understanding is the self.   42

Knowing the self beyond understanding,
sustain the self with the self.
Great Warrior, kill the enemy
menacing you in the form of desire!   43

The Fourth Teaching

KNOWLEDGE

Lord Krishna

I taught this undying discipline
to the shining sun, first of mortals,
who told it to Manu, the progenitor of man;
Manu told it to the solar king Ikshvaku.   1

Royal sages knew this discipline,
which the tradition handed down;
but over the course of time
it has decayed, Arjuna.   2

This is the ancient discipline
that I have taught to you today;
you are my devotee and my friend,
and this is the deepest mystery.   3

Arjuna

Your birth followed the birth
of the sun;
how can I comprehend that you taught it
in the beginning?   4

Lord Krishna

I have passed through many births
and so have you;
I know them all,
but you do not, Arjuna.   5

Though myself unborn, undying,
the lord of creatures, I fashion nature,
which is mine, and I come into being
through my own magic.   6

Whenever sacred duty decays
and chaos prevails,
then, I create
myself, Arjuna.   7

To protect men of virtue
and destroy men who do evil,
to set the standard of sacred duty,
I appear in age after age.   8

He who really knows my divine
birth and my action, escapes rebirth
when he abandons the body—
and he comes to me, Arjuna.   9

Free from attraction, fear, and anger,
filled with me, dependent on me,
purified by the fire of knowledge,
many come into my presence.   10

As they seek refuge in me,
I devote myself to them;
Arjuna, men retrace
my path in every way.   11

Desiring success in their actions,
men sacrifice here to the gods;
in the world of man
success comes quickly from action.   12

I created mankind in four classes,
different in their qualities and actions;
though unchanging, I am the agent of this,
the actor who never acts! 13

I desire no fruit of actions,
and actions do not defile me;
one who knows this about me
is not bound by actions. 14

Knowing this, even ancient seekers
of freedom performed action—
do as these seers
did in ancient times. 15

What is action? What is inaction?
Even the poets were confused—
what I shall teach you of action
will free you from misfortune. 16

One should understand action,
understand wrong action,
and understand inaction too;
the way of action is obscure. 17

A man who sees inaction in action
and action in inaction
has understanding among men,
disciplined in all action he performs. 18

The wise say a man is learned
when his plans lack constructs of desire,
when his actions are burned
by the fire of knowledge. 19

Abandoning attachment to fruits
of action, always content, independent,
he does nothing at all
even when he engages in action.   20

He incurs no guilt if he has no hope,
restrains his thought and himself,
abandons possessions,
and performs actions with his body only.   21

Content with whatever comes by chance,
beyond dualities, free from envy,
impartial to failure and success,
he is not bound even when he acts.   22

When a man is unattached and free,
his reason deep in knowledge,
acting only in sacrifice,
his action is wholly dissolved.   23

The infinite spirit is the offering,
the oblation it pours into infinite fire,
and the infinite spirit can be reached
by contemplating its infinite action.   24

Some men of discipline offer
sacrifice only to the gods;
others sacrifice with oblation
in the fire of infinite spirit.   25

Some offer senses such as hearing
in the fires of restraint;
others offer sound and other objects
in the fires of the senses.   26

Others offer all actions of the senses
and all actions of breath
in the fire of discipline kindled
by knowledge—the mastery of one's self.   27

Ascetics who keep strict vows
sacrifice with material objects,
through penance, discipline,
study of sacred lore, and knowledge.   28

Others sacrifice by suspending
the cycle of vital breath,
the flow of inhaling and exhaling,
as they practice breath control.   29

Others restricting their food
offer breaths in vital breaths;
all these understand sacrifice
and in sacrifice exhaust their sins.   30

Men who eat remnants of sacrifice
attain the timeless infinite spirit;
what is this world or the next
for a man without sacrifice, Arjuna?   31

Many forms of sacrifice
expand toward the infinite spirit;
know that the source of them all
is action, and you will be free.   32

Sacrifice in knowledge is better
than sacrifice with material objects;
the totality of all action
culminates in knowledge, Arjuna,   33

Know it by humble submission,
by asking questions, and by service;
wise men who see reality
will give you knowledge.   34

Arjuna, when you have realized this,
you will not descend into delusion again;
knowledge will let you see creatures
within yourself and so in me.   35

Even if you are the most evil
of all sinners,
you will cross over all evil
on the raft of knowledge.   36

Just as a flaming fire reduces
wood to ashes, Arjuna,
so the fire of knowledge
reduces all actions to ashes.   37

No purifier equals knowledge,
and in time
the man of perfect discipline
discovers this in his own spirit.   38

Faithful, intent, his senses
subdued, he gains knowledge;
gaining knowledge,
he soon finds perfect peace.   39

An ignorant man is lost, faithless,
and filled with self-doubt;
a soul that harbors doubt has no joy,
not in this world or the next.   40

Arjuna, actions do not bind
a man in possession of himself,
who renounces action through discipline
and severs doubt with knowledge.   41

So sever the ignorant doubt
in your heart with the sword
of self-knowledge, Arjuna!
Observe your discipline! Arise!   42

The Fifth Teaching

RENUNCIATION
OF ACTION

Arjuna

Krishna, you praise renunciation
of actions and then discipline;
tell me with certainty
which is the better of these two.   1

Lord Krishna

Renunciation and discipline in action
both effect good beyond measure;
but of the two, discipline in action
surpasses renunciation of action.   2

The man of eternal renunciation
is one who neither hates nor desires;
beyond dualities,
he is easily freed from bondage.   3

Simpletons separate philosophy
and discipline, but the learned do not;
applying one correctly, a man
finds the fruit of both.   4

Men of discipline reach the same place
that philosophers attain;
he really sees who sees philosophy
and discipline to be one.   5

Renunciation is difficult to attain
without discipline;
a sage armed with discipline
soon reaches the infinite spirit.   6

Armed with discipline, he purifies
and subdues the self, masters his senses,
unites himself with the self of all creatures;
even when he acts, he is not defiled.   7

Seeing, hearing, touching, smelling,
eating, walking, sleeping, breathing,
the disciplined man who knows reality
should think, "I do nothing at all."   8

When talking, giving, taking,
opening and closing his eyes,
he keeps thinking, "It is the senses
that engage in sense objects."   9

A man who relinquishes attachment
and dedicates actions to the infinite spirit
is not stained by evil,
like a lotus leaf unstained by water.   10

Relinquishing attachment,
men of discipline perform action
with body, mind, understanding, and senses
for the purification of the self.   11

Relinquishing the fruit of action,
the disciplined man attains perfect peace;
the undisciplined man is in bondage,
attached to the fruit of his desire.   12

Renouncing all actions with the mind,
the masterful embodied self
dwells at ease in its nine-gated fortress—
it neither acts nor causes action.   13

The lord of the world
does not create agency or actions,
or a union of fruits with actions;
but his being unfolds into existence.   14

The lord does not partake
of anyone's evil or good conduct;
knowledge is obscured by ignorance,
so people are deluded.   15

When ignorance is destroyed
by knowledge of the self,
then, like the sun, knowledge
illumines ultimate reality.   16

That becomes their understanding,
their self, their basis, and their goal,
and they reach a state beyond return,
their sin dispelled by knowledge.   17

Learned men see with an equal eye
a scholarly and dignified priest,
a cow, an elephant, a dog,
and even an outcaste scavenger.   18

Men who master the worldly world
have equanimity—
they exist in the infinite spirit,
in its flawless equilibrium.   19

He should not rejoice in what he loves
nor recoil from what disgusts him;
secure in understanding, undeluded, knowing
the infinite spirit, he abides in it.   20

Detached from external contacts,
he discovers joy in himself;
joined by discipline to the infinite spirit,
the self attains inexhaustible joy.   21

Delights from external objects
are wombs of suffering;
in their beginning is their end,
and no wise man delights in them.   22

A man able to endure
the force of desire and anger
before giving up his body
is disciplined and joyful.   23

The man of discipline has joy,
delight, and light within;
becoming the infinite spirit,
he finds the pure calm of infinity.   24

Seers who can destroy their sins,
cut through doubt, master the self,
and delight in the good of all creatures
attain the pure calm of infinity.   25

The pure calm of infinity
exists for the ascetic
who disarms desire and anger,
controls reason, and knows the self.   26

He shuns external objects,
fixes his gaze between his brows,
and regulates his vital breaths
as they pass through his nostrils.   27

Truly free is the sage who controls
his senses, mind, and understanding,
who focuses on freedom
and dispels desire, fear, and anger.   28

Knowing me as the enjoyer
of sacrifices and penances, lord of all worlds,
and friend of all creatures,
he finds peace.   29

THE MAN OF DISCIPLINE

Lord Krishna

One who does what must be done
without concern for the fruits
is a man of renunciation and discipline,
not one who shuns ritual fire and rites.   1

Know that discipline, Arjuna,
is what men call renunciation;
no man is disciplined
without renouncing willful intent.   2

Action is the means for a sage
who seeks to mature in discipline;
tranquility is the means
for one who is mature in discipline.   3

He is said to be mature in discipline
when he has renounced all intention
and is detached
from sense objects and actions.   4

He should elevate himself by the self,
not degrade himself;
for the self is its own friend
and its own worst foe.   5

The self is the friend of a man
who masters himself through the self,
but for a man without self-mastery,
the self is like an enemy at war.   6

The higher self of a tranquil man
whose self is mastered
is perfectly poised in cold or heat,
joy or suffering, honor or contempt.   7

Self-contented in knowledge and judgment,
his senses subdued, on the summit of existence,
impartial to clay, stone, or gold,
the man of discipline is disciplined.   8

He is set apart by his disinterest
toward comrades, allies, enemies,
neutrals, nonpartisans, foes, friends,
good and even evil men.   9

A man of discipline should always
discipline himself, remain in seclusion,
isolated, his thought and self well controlled,
without possessions or hope.   10

He should fix for himself
a firm seat in a pure place,
neither too high nor too low,
covered in cloth, deerskin, or grass.   11

He should focus his mind and restrain
the activity of his thought and senses;
sitting on that seat, he should practice
discipline for the purification of the self.   12

He should keep his body, head,
and neck aligned, immobile, steady;
he should gaze at the tip of his nose
and not let his glance wander.   13

The self tranquil, his fear dispelled,
firm in his vow of celibacy, his mind restrained,
let him sit with discipline,
his thought fixed on me, intent on me.   14

Disciplining himself,
his mind controlled,
a man of discipline finds peace,
the pure calm that exists in me.   15

Gluttons have no discipline,
nor the man who starves himself,
nor he who sleeps excessively
or suffers wakefulness.   16

When a man disciplines his diet
and diversions, his physical actions,
his sleeping and waking,
discipline destroys his sorrow.   17

When his controlled thought
rests within the self alone,
without craving objects of desire,
he is said to be disciplined.   18

"He does not waver, like a lamp sheltered
from the wind" is the simile recalled
for a man of discipline, restrained in thought
and practicing self-discipline.   19

When his thought ceases,
checked by the exercise of discipline,
he is content within the self,
seeing the self through himself.   20

Absolute joy beyond the senses
can only be grasped by understanding;
when one knows it, he abides there
and never wanders from this reality.   21

Obtaining it, he thinks
there is no greater gain;
abiding there, he is unmoved,
even by deep suffering.   22

Since he knows that discipline
means unbinding the bonds of suffering,
he should practice discipline resolutely,
without despair dulling his reason.   23

He should entirely relinquish
desires aroused by willful intent;
he should entirely control
his senses with his mind.   24

He should gradually become tranquil,
firmly controlling his understanding;
focusing his mind on the self,
he should think nothing.   25

Wherever his faltering mind
unsteadily wanders,
he should restrain it
and bring it under self-control.   26

When his mind is tranquil, perfect joy
comes to the man of discipline;
his passion is calmed, he is without sin,
being one with the infinite spirit.   27

Constantly disciplining himself,
free from sin, the man of discipline
easily achieves perfect joy
in harmony with the infinite spirit.   28

Arming himself with discipline,
seeing everything with an equal eye,
he sees the self in all creatures
and all creatures in the self.   29

He who sees me everywhere
and sees everything in me
will not be lost to me,
and I will not be lost to him.   30

I exist in all creatures,
so the disciplined man devoted to me
grasps the oneness of life;
wherever he is, he is in me.   31

When he sees identity in everything,
whether joy or suffering,
through analogy with the self,
he is deemed a man of pure discipline.   32

Arjuna

You define this discipline
by equanimity, Krishna;
but in my faltering condition,
I see no ground for it.   33

Krishna, the mind is faltering,
violent, strong, and stubborn;
I find it as difficult
to hold as the wind.   34

Lord Krishna

Without doubt, the mind
is unsteady and hard to hold,
but practice and dispassion
can restrain it, Arjuna.   35

In my view, discipline eludes
the unrestrained self,
but if he strives to master himself,
a man has the means to reach it.   36

Arjuna

When a man has faith, but no ascetic will,
and his mind deviates from discipline
before its perfection is achieved,
what way is there for him, Krishna?   37

Doomed by his double failure,
is he not like a cloud split apart,
unsettled, deluded on the path
of the infinite spirit?   38

Krishna, only you can dispel
this doubt of mine completely;
there is no one but you
to dispel this doubt.   39

Lord Krishna

Arjuna, he does not suffer
doom in this world or the next;
any man who acts with honor
cannot go the wrong way, my friend.   40

Fallen in discipline, he reaches
worlds made by his virtue, wherein he dwells
for endless years, until he is reborn
in a house of upright and noble men.   41

Or he is born in a family
of disciplined men;
the kind of birth in the world
that is very hard to win.   42

There he regains a depth
of understanding from his former life
and strives further
to perfection, Arjuna.   43

Carried by the force of his previous practice,
a man who seeks to learn discipline
passes beyond sacred lore
that expresses the infinite spirit in words.   44

The man of discipline, striving
with effort, purified of his sins,
perfected through many births,
finds a higher way.   45

He is deemed superior
to men of penance,
men of knowledge, and men of action;
be a man of discipline, Arjuna!   46

Of all the men of discipline,
the faithful man devoted to me,
with his inner self deep in mine,
I deem most disciplined.   47

The Seventh Teaching

KNOWLEDGE AND JUDGMENT

Lord Krishna

Practice discipline in my protection,
with your mind focused on me;
Arjuna, hear how you can know me
completely, without doubt.   1

I will teach you the totality
of knowledge and judgment;
this known, nothing else
in the world need be known.   2

One man among thousands
strives for success,
and of the few who are successful,
a rare one knows my reality.   3

My nature has eight aspects:
earth, water, fire, wind, space,
mind, understanding,
and individuality.   4

This is my lower nature;
know my higher nature too,
the life-force
that sustains this universe.   5

Learn that this is the womb
of all creatures;
I am the source of all the universe,
just as I am its dissolution.   6

Nothing is higher than I am;
Arjuna, all that exists
is woven on me,
like a web of pearls on thread.   7

I am the taste in water, Arjuna,
the light in the moon and sun,
OM resonant in all sacred lore,
the sound in space, valor in men.   8

I am the pure fragrance
in earth, the brilliance in fire,
the life in all living creatures,
the penance in ascetics.   9

Know me, Arjuna,
as every creature's timeless seed,
the understanding of intelligent men,
the brilliance of fiery heroes.   10

Of strong men, I am strength,
without the emotion of desire;
in creatures I am the desire
that does not impede sacred duty.   11

Know that nature's qualities
come from me—lucidity,
passion, and dark inertia;
I am not in them, they are in me.   12

All this universe, deluded
by the qualities inherent in nature,
fails to know that I am
beyond them and unchanging.   13

Composed of nature's qualities,
my divine magic is hard to escape;
but those who seek refuge in me
cross over this magic.   14

Vile, deluded sinners are the men
who fail to take refuge in me;
their knowledge ruined by magic,
they fall prey to demonic power.   15

Arjuna, four types of virtuous men
are devoted to me:
the tormented man, the seeker of wisdom,
the suppliant, and the sage.   16

Of these, the disciplined man of knowledge
is set apart by his singular devotion;
I am dear to the man of knowledge,
and he is dear to me.   17

They are all noble, but I regard
the man of knowledge to be my very self;
self-disciplined, he holds me
to be the highest way.   18

At the end of many births,
the man of knowledge finds refuge in me;
he is the rare great spirit who sees
"Krishna is all that is."   19

Robbed of knowledge by stray desires,
men take refuge in other deities;
observing varied rites,
they are limited by their own nature.   20

I grant unwavering faith
to any devoted man who wants
to worship any form
with faith.   21

Disciplined by that faith,
he seeks the deity's favor;
this secured, he gains desires
that I myself grant. 22

But finite is the reward
that comes to men of little wit;
men who sacrifice to gods reach the gods;
those devoted to me reach me. 23

Men without understanding think that I am
unmanifest nature become manifest;
they are ignorant of my higher existence,
my pure, unchanging absolute being. 24

Veiled in the magic of my discipline,
I elude most men;
this deluded world is not aware
that I am unborn and immutable. 25

I know all creatures
that have been, that now exist,
and that are yet to be;
but, Arjuna, no one knows me. 26

All creatures are bewildered
at birth by the delusion
of opposing dualities
that arise from desire and hatred. 27

But when they cease from evil
and act with virtue, they devote
themselves to me, firm in their vows,
freed from the delusion of duality. 28

Trusting me, men strive
for freedom from old age and death;
they know the infinite spirit,
its inner self and all its action. 29

Men who know me as its inner being,
inner divinity, and inner sacrifice
have disciplined their reason;
they know me at the time of death.   30

The Eighth Teaching

THE INFINITE SPIRIT

Arjuna

What is the infinite spirit, Krishna?
What is its inner self, its action?
What is its inner being called?
What is its inner divinity?   1

Who is within sacrifice, Krishna?
How is he here in the body?
And how are men of self-control
to know you at the time of death?   2

Lord Krishna

Eternal and supreme is the infinite spirit;
its inner self is called inherent being;
its creative force, known as action,
is the source of creatures' existence.   3

Its inner being is perishable existence;
its inner divinity is man's spirit;
I am the inner sacrifice
here in your body, O Best of Mortals.   4

A man who dies remembering me
at the time of death enters my being
when he is freed from his body;
of this there is no doubt.   5

Whatever being he remembers
when he abandons the body at death,
he enters, Arjuna,
always existing in that being.   6

Therefore, at all times remember me
and fight;
mind and understanding fixed on me,
free from doubt, you will come to me.   7

Disciplined through practice,
his reason never straying,
meditating, one reaches
the supreme divine spirit of man.   8

One should remember
man's spirit as the guide,
the primordial poet,
smaller than an atom,
granter of all things,
in form inconceivable,
the color of the sun
beyond darkness.   9

At the time of death,
with the mind immovable,
armed with devotion
and strength of discipline,
focusing vital breath
between the brows,
one attains the supreme
divine spirit of man.   10

I shall teach you,
in summary,
about the state
that scholars of sacred lore
call eternal,
the state ascetics enter,
freed from passion,
which some men seek
in the celibate life.   11

Controlling the body's gates,
keeping the mind in the heart,
holding his own breath in his head,
one is in disciplined concentration.   12

Invoking the infinite spirit
as the one eternal syllable OM,
remembering me as he abandons his body,
he reaches the absolute way.   13

When he constantly remembers me,
focusing his reason on me,
I am easy to reach, Arjuna,
for the man of enduring discipline.   14

Reaching me, men of great spirit
do not undergo rebirth,
the ephemeral realm of suffering;
they attain absolute perfection.   15

Even in Brahma's cosmic realm
worlds evolve in incessant cycles,
but a man who reaches me
suffers no rebirth, Arjuna.   16

When they know that a day of Brahma
stretches over a thousand eons,
and his night ends in a thousand eons,
men understand day and night.   17

At break of Brahma's day
all things emerge from unmanifest nature;
when night falls, all sink
into unmanifest darkness.   18

Arjuna, the throng of creatures
that comes to exist dissolves
unwillingly at nightfall
to emerge again at daybreak.   19

Beyond this unmanifest nature
is another unmanifest existence,
a timeless being that does not perish
when all creatures perish.   20

It is called eternal unmanifest nature,
what men call the highest way,
the goal from which they do not return;
this highest realm is mine.   21

It is man's highest spirit,
won by singular devotion, Arjuna,
in whom creatures rest
and the whole universe extends.   22

Arjuna, I shall tell you precisely
the time when men of discipline
who have died
suffer rebirth or escape it.   23

Men who know the infinite spirit
reach its infinity if they die
in fire, light, day, bright lunar night,
the sun's six-month northward course.   24

In smoke, night, dark lunar night,
the sun's six-month southward course,
a man of discipline
reaches the moon's light and returns.   25

These bright and dark pathways
are deemed constant for the universe;
by one, a man escapes rebirth;
by the other, he is born again.   26

No man of discipline is deluded
when he knows these two paths.
Therefore, Arjuna, be armed
in all times with discipline.   27

Knowing the fruit of virtue
assigned to knowledge of sacred lore,
to sacrifices, to penances,
and to acts of charity,
the man of discipline
transcends all this
and ascends to the place
of pure beginning.   28

The Ninth Teaching

THE SUBLIME MYSTERY

Lord Krishna

I will teach the deepest mystery
to you since you find no fault;
realizing it with knowledge and judgment,
you will be free from misfortune.   1

This science and mystery of kings
is the supreme purifier,
intuitive, true to duty,
joyous to perform, unchanging.   2

Without faith in sacred duty,
men fail to reach me, Arjuna;
they return to the cycle
of death and rebirth.   3

The whole universe is pervaded
by my unmanifest form;
all creatures exist in me,
but I do not exist in them.   4

Behold the power of my discipline;
these creatures are really not in me;
my self quickens creatures,
sustaining them without being in them.   5

Just as the wide-moving wind
is constantly present in space,
so all creatures exist in me;
understand it to be so!   6

As an eon ends, all creatures
fold into my nature, Arjuna;
and I create them again
as a new eon begins.   7

Gathering in my own nature,
again and again I freely create
this whole throng of creatures,
helpless in the force of my nature.   8

These actions do not bind me,
since I remain detached
in all my actions, Arjuna,
as if I stood apart from them.   9

Nature, with me as her inner eye,
bears animate and inanimate beings;
and by reason of this, Arjuna,
the universe continues to turn.   10

Deluded men despise me
in the human form I have assumed,
ignorant of my higher existence
as the great lord of creatures.   11

Reason warped, hope, action,
and knowledge wasted,
they fall prey to a seductive
fiendish, demonic nature.   12

In single-minded dedication, great souls
devote themselves to my divine nature,
knowing me as unchanging,
the origin of creatures.   13

Always glorifying me,
striving, firm in their vows,
paying me homage with devotion,
they worship me, always disciplined.   14

Sacrificing through knowledge,
others worship my universal presence
in its unity
and in its many different aspects.   15

I am the rite, the sacrifice,
the libation for the dead, the healing herb,
the sacred hymn, the clarified butter,
the fire, the oblation.   16

I am the universal father,
mother, granter of all, grandfather,
object of knowledge, purifier,
holy syllable OM, threefold sacred lore.   17

I am the way, sustainer, lord,
witness, shelter, refuge, friend,
source, dissolution, stability,
treasure, and unchanging seed.   18

I am heat that withholds
and sends down the rains;
I am immortality and death;
both being and nonbeing am I.   19

Men learned in sacred lore,
Soma drinkers, their sins absolved,
worship me with sacrifices,
seeking to win heaven.
Reaching the holy world of Indra,
king of the gods,
they savor the heavenly delights
of the gods in the celestial sphere.   20

When they have long enjoyed
the world of heaven
and their merit is exhausted,
they enter the mortal world;
following the duties
ordained in sacred lore,
desiring desires,
they obtain what is transient.   21

Men who worship me,
thinking solely of me,
always disciplined,
win the reward I secure.   22

When devoted men sacrifice
to other deities with faith,
they sacrifice to me, Arjuna,
however aberrant the rites.   23

I am the enjoyer
and the lord of all sacrifices;
they do not know me in reality,
and so they fail.   24

Votaries of the gods go to the gods,
ancestor-worshippers go to the ancestors,
those who propitiate ghosts go to them,
and my worshippers go to me.   25

The leaf or flower or fruit or water
that he offers with devotion,
I take from the man of self-restraint
in response to his devotion.   26

Whatever you do—what you take,
what you offer, what you give,
what penances you perform—
do as an offering to me, Arjuna!   27

You will be freed from the bonds of action,
from the fruit of fortune and misfortune;
armed with the discipline of renunciation,
your self liberated, you will join me.   28

I am impartial to all creatures,
and no one is hateful or dear to me;
but men devoted to me are in me,
and I am within them.   29

If he is devoted solely to me,
even a violent criminal
must be deemed a man of virtue,
for his resolve is right.   30

His spirit quickens to sacred duty,
and he finds eternal peace;
Arjuna, know that no one
devoted to me is lost.   31

If they rely on me, Arjuna,
women, commoners, men of low rank,
even men born in the womb of evil,
reach the highest way.   32

How easy it is then for holy priests
and devoted royal sages—
in this transient world of sorrow,
devote yourself to me!   33

Keep me in your mind and devotion,
sacrifice to me, bow to me,
discipline your self toward me,
and you will reach me!   34

The Tenth Teaching

FRAGMENTS OF
DIVINE POWER

Lord Krishna

Great Warrior, again hear
my word in its supreme form;
desiring your good,
I speak to deepen your love.   1

Neither the multitude of gods
nor great sages know my origin,
for I am the source of all
the gods and great sages.   2

A mortal who knows me
as the unborn, beginningless
great lord of the worlds
is freed from delusion and all evils.   3

Understanding, knowledge, nondelusion,
patience, truth, control, tranquility,
joy, suffering, being, nonbeing,
fear, and fearlessness . . .   4

Nonviolence, equanimity, contentment,
penance, charity, glory, disgrace,
these diverse attitudes
of creatures' arise from me.   5

The seven ancient great sages
and the four ancestors of man
are mind-born aspects of me;
their progeny fills the world.   6

The man who in reality knows
my power and my discipline
is armed with unwavering discipline;
in this there is no doubt.   7

I am the source of everything,
and everything proceeds from me;
filled with my existence, wise men
realizing this are devoted to me.   8

Thinking and living deep in me,
they enlighten one another
by constantly telling of me
for their own joy and delight.   9

To men of enduring discipline,
devoted to me with affection,
I give the discipline of understanding
by which they come to me.   10

Dwelling compassionately
deep in the self,
I dispel darkness born of ignorance
with the radiant light of knowledge.   11

Arjuna

You are supreme, the infinite spirit,
the highest abode, sublime purifier,
man's spirit, eternal, divine,
the primordial god, unborn, omnipotent.   12

So the ancient seers spoke of you,
as did the epic poet Vyasa and the bards
who sang for gods, ancestors, and men;
and now you tell me yourself.   13

Lord Krishna, I realize the truth
of all you tell me;
neither gods nor demons
know your manifest nature.   14

You know yourself through the self,
Krishna; Supreme among Men,
Sustainer and Lord of Creatures,
God of Gods, Master of the Universe!   15

Tell me without reserve
the divine powers of your self,
powers by which you pervade
these worlds.   16

Lord of Discipline,
how can I know you as I meditate
on you—in what diverse aspects
can I think of you, Krishna?   17

Recount in full extent
the discipline and power of your self;
Krishna, I can never hear enough
of your immortal speech.   18

Lord Krishna

Listen, Arjuna, as I recount
for you in essence
the divine powers of my self;
endless is my extent.   19

I am the self abiding
in the heart of all creatures;
I am their beginning,
their middle, and their end.   20

I am Vishnu striding among sun gods,
the radiant sun among lights;
I am lightning among wind gods,
the moon among the stars.   21

I am the song in sacred lore;
I am Indra, king of the gods;
I am the mind of the senses,
the consciousness of creatures.   22

I am gracious Shiva among howling storm gods,
the lord of wealth among demigods and demons,
fire blazing among the bright gods;
I am golden Meru towering over the mountains.   23

Arjuna, know me as the gods' teacher,
chief of the household priests;
I am the god of war among generals;
I am the ocean of lakes.   24

I am Bhrigu, priest of the great seers;
of words, I am the eternal syllable OM,
the prayer of sacrifices;
I am Himalaya, the measure of what endures.   25

Among trees, I am the sacred fig-tree;
I am chief of the divine sages,
leader of the celestial musicians,
the recluse philosopher among saints.   26

Among horses, know me as the immortal stallion
born from the sea of elixir;
among elephants, the divine king's mount;
among men, the king.   27

I am the thunderbolt among weapons,
among cattle, the magical wish-granting cow;
I am the procreative god of love,
the king of the snakes.   28

I am the endless cosmic serpent,
the lord of all sea creatures;
I am chief of the ancestral fathers;
of restraints, I am death.   29

I am the pious son of demons;
of measures, I am time;
I am the lion among wild animals,
the eagle among birds.   30

I am the purifying wind,
the warrior Rama bearing arms,
the sea-monster crocodile,
the flowing river Ganges.   31

I am the beginning, the middle,
and the end of creations, Arjuna;
of sciences, I am the science of the self;
I am the dispute of orators.   32

I am the vowel *a* of the syllabary,
the pairing of words in a compound;
I am indestructible time,
the creator facing everywhere at once.   33

I am death the destroyer of all,
the source of what will be,
the feminine powers: fame, fortune, speech,
memory, intelligence, resolve, patience.   34

I am the great ritual chant,
the meter of sacred song,
the most sacred month in the year,
the spring blooming with flowers.   35

I am the dice game of gamblers,
the brilliance of fiery heroes.
I am victory and resolve,
the lucidity of lucid men.   36

I am Krishna among my mighty kinsmen;
I am Arjuna among the Pandava princes;
I am the epic poet Vyasa among sages,
the inspired singer among bards.   37

I am the scepter of rulers,
the morality of ambitious men;
I am the silence of mysteries,
what men of knowledge know.   38

Arjuna, I am the seed
of all creatures;
nothing animate or inanimate
could exist without me.   39

Fiery Hero, endless
are my divine powers—
of my power's extent
I have barely hinted.   40

Whatever is powerful, lucid,
splendid, or invulnerable
has its source in a fragment
of my brilliance.   41

What use is so much knowledge
to you, Arjuna?
I stand sustaining this entire world
with a fragment of my being.   42

THE VISION OF KRISHNA'S TOTALITY

Arjuna

To favor me you revealed
the deepest mystery of the self,
and by your words
my delusion is dispelled.   1

I heard from you in detail
how creatures come to be and die,
Krishna, and about the self
in its immutable greatness.   2

Just as you have described
yourself, I wish to see your form
in all its majesty,
Krishna, Supreme among Men.   3

If you think I can see it,
reveal to me
your immutable self,
Krishna, Lord of Discipline.   4

Lord Krishna

Arjuna, see my forms
in hundreds and thousands;
diverse, divine,
of many colors and shapes.   5

See the sun gods, gods of light,
howling storm gods, twin gods of dawn,
and gods of wind, Arjuna,
wondrous forms not seen before.   6

Arjuna, see all the universe,
animate and inanimate,
and whatever else you wish to see;
all stands here as one in my body.   7

But you cannot see me
with your own eye;
I will give you a divine eye to see
the majesty of my discipline.   8

Sanjaya

O King, saying this, Krishna,
the great lord of discipline,
revealed to Arjuna
the true majesty of his form.   9

It was a multiform, wondrous vision,
with countless mouths and eyes
and celestial ornaments,
brandishing many divine weapons.   10

Everywhere was boundless divinity
containing all astonishing things,
wearing divine garlands and garments,
annointed with divine perfume.   11

If the light of a thousand suns
were to rise in the sky at once,
it would be like the light
of that great spirit.   12

Arjuna saw all the universe
in its many ways and parts,
standing as one in the body
of the god of gods.   13

Then filled with amazement,
his hair bristling on his flesh,
Arjuna bowed his head to the god,
joined his hands in homage, and spoke.   14

Arjuna

I see the gods
in your body, O God,
and hordes
of varied creatures:
Brahma, the cosmic creator,
on his lotus throne,
all the seers
and celestial serpents.   15

I see your boundless form
everywhere,
the countless arms,
bellies, mouths, and eyes;
Lord of All,
I see no end,
or middle or beginning
to your totality.   16

I see you blazing
through the fiery rays
of your crown, mace, and discus,
hard to behold
in the burning light
of fire and sun
that surrounds
your measureless presence.   17

You are to be known
as supreme eternity,
the deepest treasure
of all that is,
the immutable guardian
of enduring sacred duty;
I think you are
man's timeless spirit.   18

I see no beginning
or middle or end to you;
only boundless strength
in your endless arms,
the moon and sun in your eyes,
your mouths of consuming flames,
your own brilliance
scorching this universe.   19

You alone
fill the space
between heaven and earth
and all the directions;
seeing this awesome,
terrible form of yours,
Great Soul,
the three worlds
tremble.   20

Throngs of gods enter you,
some in their terror
make gestures of homage
to invoke you;
throngs of great sages
and saints
hail you and praise you
in resounding hymns.   21

Howling storm gods, sun gods,
bright gods, and gods of ritual,
gods of the universe,
twin gods of dawn, wind gods,
vapor-drinking ghosts,
throngs of celestial musicians,
demigods, demons, and saints,
all gaze at you amazed.   22

Seeing the many mouths
and eyes
of your great form,
its many arms,
thighs, feet,
bellies, and fangs,
the worlds tremble
and so do I.   23

Vishnu, seeing you brush
the clouds with flames
of countless colors,
your mouths agape,
your huge eyes blazing,
my inner self quakes
and I find no resolve
or tranquility.   24

Seeing the fangs
protruding
from your mouths
like the fires of time,
I lose my bearings
and I find no refuge;
be gracious, Lord of Gods,
Shelter of the Universe.   25

All those sons
of the blind king
Dhritarashtra
come accompanied
by troops of kings,
by the generals Bhishma,
Drona, Karna,
and by our battle leaders.   26

Rushing through
your fangs
into grim
mouths,
some are dangling
from heads
crushed
between your teeth.   27

As roiling
river waters
stream headlong
toward the sea,
so do these human
heroes enter
into your blazing
mouths.   28

As moths
in the frenzy
of destruction
fly into a blazing flame,
worlds
in the frenzy
of destruction
enter your mouths.   29

You lick at the worlds
around you,
devouring them
with flaming mouths;
and your terrible fires
scorch the entire universe,
filling it, Vishnu,
with violent rays.   30

Tell me—
who are you
in this terrible form?
Homage to you, Best of Gods!
Be gracious! I want to know you
as you are in your beginning.
I do not comprehend
the course of your ways.   31

Lord Krishna

I am time grown old,
creating world destruction,
set in motion
to annihilate the worlds;
even without you,
all these warriors
arrayed in hostile ranks
will cease to exist.   32

Therefore, arise
and win glory!
Conquer your foes
and fulfill your kingship!
They are already
killed by me.
Be just my instrument,
the archer at my side!   33

Drona, Bhishma, Jayadratha,
and Karna,
and all the other battle heroes,
are killed by me.
Kill them
without wavering;
fight, and you will conquer
your foes in battle!   34

Sanjaya

Hearing Krishna's words,
Arjuna trembled
under his crown,
and he joined his hands
in reverent homage;
terrified of his fear,
he bowed to Krishna
and stammered in reply.   35

Arjuna

Krishna, the universe
responds
with joy and rapture
to your glory,
terrified demons
flee in far directions,
and saints throng
to bow in homage.   36

Why should they not bow
in homage to you, Great Soul,
Original Creator,
more venerable than the creator Brahma?
Boundless Lord of Gods,
Shelter of All That Is,
you are eternity,
being, nonbeing, and beyond.   37

You are the original god,
the primordial spirit of man,
the deepest treasure
of all that is,
knower and what is to be known,
the supreme abode;
you pervade the universe,
Lord of Boundless Form.   38

You are the gods of wind,
death, fire, and water;
the moon; the lord of life;
and the great ancestor.
Homage to you,
a thousand times homage!
I bow in homage to you
again and yet again.   39

I bow in homage
before you and behind you;
I bow everywhere
to your omnipresence!
You have boundless strength
and limitless force;
you fulfill
all that you are.   40

Thinking you a friend,
I boldly said,
"Welcome, Krishna!
Welcome, cousin, friend!"
From negligence,
or through love,
I failed to know
your greatness.   41

If in jest
I offended you,
alone
or publicly,
at sport, rest,
sitting, or at meals,
I beg your patience,
unfathomable Krishna.   42

You are father of the world
of animate and inanimate things,
its venerable teacher,
most worthy of worship,
without equal.
Where in all three worlds
is another to match
your extraordinary power?   43

I bow to you,
I prostrate my body,
I beg you to be gracious,
Worshipful Lord—
as a father to a son,
a friend to a friend,
a lover to a beloved,
O God, bear with me.   44

I am thrilled,
and yet my mind
trembles with fear
at seeing
what has not been seen before.
Show me, God, the form I know—
be gracious, Lord of Gods,
Shelter of the World.   45

I want to see you
as before,
with your crown and mace,
and the discus in your hand.
O Thousand-Armed God,
assume the four-armed form
embodied
in your totality.   46

Lord Krishna

To grace you, Arjuna,
I revealed
through self-discipline
my higher form,
which no one but you
has ever beheld—
brilliant, total,
boundless, primal.   47

Not through sacred lore
or sacrificial ritual
or study or charity,
not by rites
or by terrible penances
can I be seen in this form
in the world of men
by anyone but you, Great Hero.   48

Do not tremble
or suffer confusion
from seeing
my horrific form;
your fear dispelled,
your mind full of love,
see my form again
as it was.   49

Sanjaya

Saying this to Arjuna,
Krishna once more
revealed
his intimate form;
resuming his gentle body,
the great spirit
let the terrified hero
regain his breath.   50

Arjuna

Seeing your gentle human form,
Krishna, I recover
my own nature,
and my reason is restored.   51

Lord Krishna

This form you have seen
is rarely revealed;
the gods are constantly craving
for a vision of this form.   52

Not through sacred lore,
penances, charity, or sacrificial rites
can I be seen in the form
that you saw me.   53

By devotion alone
can I, as I really am,
be known and seen
and entered into, Arjuna.   54

Acting only for me, intent on me,
free from attachment,
hostile to no creature, Arjuna,
a man of devotion comes to me.   55

The Twelfth Teaching

DEVOTION

Arjuna

Who best knows discipline:
men who worship you with devotion,
ever disciplined, or men who worship
the imperishable, unmanifest?

1

Lord Krishna

I deem most disciplined
men of enduring discipline
who worship me with true faith,
entrusting their minds to me.

2

Men reach me too who worship
what is imperishable, ineffable, unmanifest,
omnipresent, inconceivable,
immutable at the summit of existence.

3

Mastering their senses,
with equanimity toward everything,
they reach me, rejoicing
in the welfare of all creatures.

4

It is more arduous when their reason
clings to my unmanifest nature;
for men constrained by bodies,
the unmanifest way is hard to attain.

5

But men intent on me
renounce all actions to me
and worship me, meditating
with singular discipline.   6

When they entrust reason to me,
Arjuna, I soon arise
to rescue them from the ocean
of death and rebirth.   7

Focus your mind on me,
let your understanding enter me;
then you will dwell
in me without doubt.   8

If you cannot concentrate
your thought firmly on me,
then seek to reach me, Arjuna,
by discipline in practice.   9

Even if you fail in practice,
dedicate yourself to action;
performing actions for my sake,
you will achieve success.   10

If you are powerless to do
even this, rely on my discipline,
be self-controlled,
and reject all fruit of action.   11

Knowledge is better than practice,
meditation better than knowledge,
rejecting fruits of action
is better still—it brings peace.   12

One who bears hate for no creature
is friendly, compassionate, unselfish,
free of individuality, patient,
the same in suffering and joy.   13

Content always, disciplined,
self-controlled, firm in his resolve,
his mind and understanding dedicated to me,
devoted to me, he is dear to me.   14

The world does not flee from him,
nor does he flee from the world;
free of delight, rage, fear,
and disgust, he is dear to me.   15

Disinterested, pure, skilled,
indifferent, untroubled,
relinquishing all involvements,
devoted to me, he is dear to me.   16

He does not rejoice or hate,
grieve or feel desire;
relinquishing fortune and misfortune,
the man of devotion is dear to me.   17

Impartial to foe and friend,
honor and contempt,
cold and heat, joy and suffering,
he is free from attachment.   18

Neutral to blame and praise,
silent, content with his fate,
unsheltered, firm in thought,
the man of devotion is dear to me.   19

Even more dear to me are devotees
who cherish this elixir of sacred duty
as I have taught it,
intent on me in their faith.   20

The Thirteenth Teaching

KNOWING THE FIELD

Lord Krishna

The field denotes
this body, and wise men
call one who knows it
the field-knower.   1

Know me as the field-knower
in all fields—what I deem
to be knowledge is knowledge
of the field and its knower.   2

Hear from me in summary
what the field is
in its character and changes,
and of the field-knower's power.   3

Ancient seers have sung of this
in many ways, with varied meters
and with aphorisms on the infinite spirit
laced with logical arguments.   4

The field contains the great elements,
individuality, understanding,
unmanifest nature, the eleven senses,
and the five sense realms.   5

Longing, hatred, happiness, suffering,
bodily form, consciousness, resolve,
thus is this field with its changes
defined in summary.   6

Knowledge means humility,
sincerity, nonviolence, patience,
honesty, reverence for one's teacher,
purity, stability, self-restraint;   7

Dispassion toward sense objects
and absence of individuality,
seeing the defects in birth, death,
old age, sickness, and suffering;   8

Detachment, uninvolvement
with sons, wife, and home,
constant equanimity
in fulfillment and frustration;   9

Unwavering devotion to me
with singular discipline;
retreating to a place of solitude,
avoiding worldly affairs;   10

Persistence in knowing the self,
seeing what knowledge of reality means—
all this is called knowledge,
the opposite is ignorance.   11

I shall teach you what is to be known;
for knowing it, one attains immortality;
it is called the supreme infinite spirit,
beginningless, neither being nor nonbeing.   12

Its hands and feet reach everywhere;
its head and face see in every direction;
hearing everything, it remains
in the world, enveloping all.   13

Lacking all the sense organs,
it shines in their qualities;
unattached, it supports everything;
without qualities, it enjoys them.   14

Outside and within all creatures,
inanimate but still animate,
too subtle to be known,
it is far distant, yet near.   15

Undivided, it seems divided
among creatures;
understood as their sustainer,
it devours and creates them.   16

The light of lights
beyond darkness it is called;
knowledge attained by knowledge,
fixed in the heart of everyone.   17

So, in summary I have explained
the field and knowledge of it;
a man devoted to me, knowing this,
enters into my being.   18

Know that both nature
and man's spirit have no beginning,
that qualities and changes
have their origin in nature.   19

For its agency in producing effects,
nature is called a cause;
in the experience of joy and suffering,
man's spirit is called a cause.   20

Man's spirit is set in nature,
experiencing the qualities born of nature;
its attachment to the qualities causes
births in the wombs of good and evil.   21

Witness, consenter, sustainer,
enjoyer—the great lord
is called the highest self,
man's true spirit in this body.   22

Knowing nature and the spirit of man,
as well as the qualities of nature,
one is not born again—
no matter how one now exists.   23

By meditating on the self, some men
see the self through the self;
others see by philosophical discipline;
others by the discipline of action.   24

Others, despite their ignorance,
revere what they hear from other men;
they too cross beyond death,
intent on what they hear.   25

Arjuna, know that anything
inanimate or alive with motion
is born from the union
of the field and its knower.   26

He really sees
who sees the highest lord
standing equal among all creatures,
undecaying amid destruction.   27

Seeing the lord standing
the same everywhere,
the self cannot injure itself
and goes the highest way.   28

He really sees who sees
that all actions are performed
by nature alone and that the self
is not an actor.   29

When he perceives the unity
existing in separate creatures
and how they expand from unity,
he attains the infinite spirit.   30

Beginningless, without qualities,
the supreme self is unchanging;
even abiding in a body, Arjuna,
it does not act, nor is it defiled.   31

Just as all-pervading space
remains unsullied in its subtlety,
so the self in every body
remains unsullied.   32

Just as one sun
illumines this entire world,
so the master of the field
illumines the entire field.   33

They reach the highest state
who with the eye of knowledge know
the boundary between the knower and its field,
and the freedom creatures have from nature.   34

The Fourteenth Teaching

THE TRIAD OF NATURE'S QUALITIES

Lord Krishna

I shall teach you still more
of the farthest knowledge one can know;
knowing it, all the sages
have reached perfection.   1

Resorting to this knowledge,
they follow the ways of my sacred duty;
in creation they are not reborn,
in dissolution they suffer no sorrow.   2

My womb is the great infinite spirit;
in it I place the embryo,
and from this, Arjuna,
comes the origin of all creatures.   3

The infinite spirit is the great womb
of all forms that come to be
in all wombs,
and I am the seed-giving father.   4

Lucidity, passion, dark inertia—
these qualities inherent in nature
bind the unchanging
embodied self in the body.   5

Lucidity, being untainted,
is luminous and without decay;
it binds one with attachment
to joy and knowledge, Arjuna.   6

Know that passion is emotional,
born of craving and attachment;
it binds the embodied self
with attachment to action.   7

Know dark inertia born of ignorance
as the delusion of every embodied self;
it binds one with negligence,
indolence, and sleep, Arjuna.   8

Lucidity addicts one to joy,
and passion to actions,
but dark inertia obscures knowledge
and addicts one to negligence.   9

When lucidity dominates
passion and inertia, it thrives;
and likewise when passion or inertia
dominates the other two.   10

When the light of knowledge
shines in all the body's senses,
then one knows
that lucidity prevails.   11

When passion increases, Arjuna,
greed and activity,
involvement in actions,
disquiet, and longing arise.   12

When dark inertia increases,
obscurity and inactivity,
negligence
and delusion, arise.   13

When lucidity prevails,
the self whose body dies
enters the untainted worlds
of those who know reality.   14

When he dies in passion,
he is born among lovers of action;
so when he dies in dark inertia,
he is born into wombs of folly.   15

The fruit of good conduct
is pure and untainted they say,
but suffering is the fruit of passion,
ignorance the fruit of dark inertia.   16

From lucidity knowledge is born;
from passion comes greed;
from dark inertia come negligence,
delusion, and ignorance.   17

Men who are lucid go upward;
men of passion stay in between;
men of dark inertia,
caught in vile ways, sink low.   18

When a man of vision sees
nature's qualities as the agent
of action and knows what lies beyond,
he enters into my being.   19

Transcending the three qualities
that are the body's source, the self
achieves immortality, freed from the sorrows
of birth, death, and old age.   20

Arjuna

Lord, what signs mark a man
who passes beyond the three qualities?
What does he do to cross
beyond these qualities?   21

Krishna

He does not dislike light
or activity or delusion;
when they cease to exist
he does not desire them.   22

He remains disinterested,
unmoved by qualities of nature;
he never wavers, knowing
that only qualities are in motion.   23

Self-reliant, impartial to suffering
and joy, to clay, stone, or gold,
the resolute man is the same
to foe and friend, to blame and praise.   24

The same in honor and disgrace,
to ally and enemy, a man
who abandons involvements
transcends the qualities of nature.   25

One who serves me faithfully,
with discipline of devotion,
transcends the qualities of nature
and shares in the infinite spirit.   26

I am the infinite spirit's foundation,
immortal and immutable,
the basis of eternal sacred duty
and of perfect joy.

27

The Fifteenth Teaching

THE TRUE SPIRIT
OF MAN

Lord Krishna

Roots in the air, branches below,
the tree of life is unchanging,
they say; its leaves are hymns,
and he who knows it knows sacred lore.   1

Its branches
stretch below and above,
nourished by nature's qualities,
budding with sense objects;
aerial roots
tangled in actions
reach downward
into the world of men.   2

Its form is unknown
here in the world;
unknown are its end,
its beginning, its extent;
cut down this tree
that has such deep roots
with the sharp ax
of detachment.   3

Then search to find
the realm
that one enters
without returning:
"I seek refuge
in the original spirit of man,
from which primordial
activity extended."

4

Without pride or delusion,
the fault of attachment overcome,
intent on the self within,
their desires extinguished,
freed from dualities,
from joy and suffering,
undeluded men
reach that realm beyond change.

5

Neither sun nor moon
nor fire illumines
my highest abode—
once there, they do not return.

6

A fragment of me in the living world
is the timeless essence of life;
it draws out the senses
and the mind inherent in nature.

7

When the lord takes on a body
and then leaves it,
he carries these along, like the wind
bearing scents from earth.   8

Governing hearing, sight,
touch, taste, smell,
and thought, he savors
objects of the senses.   9

Deluded men do not perceive him
in departure or presence
or enjoyment of nature's qualities;
but the eyes of knowledge see him.   10

Men of discipline who strive
see him present within themselves;
but without self-mastery and reason,
even those who strive fail to see.   11

Know that my brilliance,
flaming in the sun,
in the moon, and in fire,
illumines this whole universe.   12

I penetrate the earth
and sustain creatures by my strength;
becoming Soma, the liquid of moonlight,
I nurture all healing herbs.   13

I am the universal fire
within the body of living beings;
I work with the flow of vital breath
to digest the foods that men consume.   14

I dwell deep
in the heart of everyone;
memory, knowledge,
and reasoning come from me;
I am the object to be known
through all sacred lore;
and I am its knower,
the creator of its final truth.   15

There is a double spirit of man
in the world, transient and eternal—
transient in all creatures,
eternal at the summit of existence.   16

Other is the supreme spirit of man,
called the supreme self,
the immutable lord who enters
and sustains the three worlds.   17

Since I transcend what is transient
and I am higher than the eternal,
I am known as the supreme spirit of man
in the world and in sacred lore.   18

Whoever knows me without delusion
as the supreme spirit of man
knows all there is, Arjuna—
he devotes his whole being to me.   19

Arjuna, thus I have taught
this most secret tradition;
realizing it, one has understanding
and his purpose is fulfilled.   20

THE DIVINE AND THE DEMONIC IN MAN

Lord Krishna

Fearlessness, purity, determination
in the discipline of knowledge,
charity, self-control, sacrifice,
study of sacred lore, penance, honesty;   1

Nonviolence, truth, absence of anger,
disengagement, peace, loyalty,
compassion for creatures, lack of greed,
gentleness, modesty, reliability;   2

Brilliance, patience, resolve,
clarity, absence of envy and of pride;
these characterize a man
born with divine traits.   3

Hypocrisy, arrogance, vanity,
anger, harshness, ignorance;
these characterize a man
born with demonic traits.   4

The divine traits lead to freedom,
the demonic lead to bondage;
do not despair, Arjuna;
you were born with the divine.   5

All creatures in the world
are either divine or demonic;
I described the divine at length;
hear what I say of the demonic.   6

Demonic men cannot comprehend
activity and rest;
there exists no clarity,
no morality, no truth in them. 7

They say that the world
has no truth, no basis, no god,
that no power of mutual dependence
is its cause, but only desire. 8

Mired in this view, lost to themselves
with their meager understanding,
these fiends contrive terrible acts
to destroy the world. 9

Subject to insatiable desire,
drunk with hypocrisy and pride,
holding false notions from delusion,
they act with impure vows. 10

In their certainty that life
consists in sating their desires,
they suffer immeasurable anxiety
that ends only with death. 11

Bound by a hundred fetters of hope,
obsessed by desire and anger,
they hoard wealth in stealthy ways
to satisfy their desires. 12

"I have gained this wish today,
and I shall attain that one;
this wealth is mine,
and there will be more. 13

I have killed that enemy,
and I shall kill others too;
I am the lord, I am the enjoyer,
successful, strong, and happy. 14

I am wealthy, and wellborn,
without peer,
I shall sacrifice, give, rejoice."
So say men deluded by ignorance. 15

Confused by endless thoughts,
caught in the net of delusion,
given to satisfying their desires,
they fall into hell's foul abyss.   16

Self-aggrandizing, stubborn,
drunk with wealth and pride,
they sacrifice in name only,
in hypocrisy, violating all norms.   17

Submitting to individuality, power,
arrogance, desire, and anger,
they hate me and revile me
in their own bodies, as in others.   18

These hateful, cruel, vile
men of misfortune, I cast
into demonic wombs
through cycles of rebirth.   19

Fallen into a demonic womb,
deluded in birth after birth,
they fail to reach me, Arjuna,
and they go the lowest way.   20

The three gates of hell
that destroy the self
are desire, anger, and greed;
one must relinquish all three.   21

Released through these three gates
of darkness, Arjuna,
a man elevates the self
and ascends to the highest way.   22

If he rejects norms of tradition
and lives to fulfill his desires,
he does not reach perfection
or happiness or the highest way.   23

Let tradition be your standard
in judging what to do or avoid;
knowing the norms of tradition,
perform your action here.   24

THREE ASPECTS
OF FAITH

Arjuna

Men who ignore the ways of tradition
but sacrifice in full faith, Krishna,
what quality of nature is basic in them—
lucidity, passion, or dark inertia?　　　　1

Lord Krishna

Listen as I explain
the threefold nature of faith
inherent in the embodied self—
lucid, passionate, and darkly inert.　　　　2

The faith each man has, Arjuna,
follows his degree of lucidity;
a man consists of his faith,
and as his faith is, so is he.　　　　3

Men of lucidity sacrifice to the gods;
men of passion, to spirits and demons;
the others, men of dark inertia,
sacrifice to corpses and to ghosts.　　　　4

Men who practice horrific penances
that go against traditional norms
are trapped in hypocrisy and individuality,
overwhelmed by the emotion of desire.　　　　5

Without reason, they torment
the elements composing their bodies,
and they torment me within them;
know them to have demonic resolve.   6

Food is also of three kinds,
to please each type of taste;
sacrifice, penance, and charity
likewise divide in three ways.   7

Foods that please lucid men
are savory, smooth, firm, and rich;
they promote long life, lucidity,
strength, health, pleasure, and delight.   8

Passionate men crave foods
that are bitter, sour, salty, hot,
pungent, harsh, and burning,
causing pain, grief, and sickness.   9

The food that pleases
men of dark inertia is stale,
unsavory, putrid, and spoiled,
leavings unfit for sacrifice.   10

A sacrifice is offered with lucidity
when the norms are kept and the mind
is focused on the sacrificial act,
without craving for its fruit.   11

But a sacrifice is offered
with passion, Arjuna,
when it is focused on the fruit
and hypocrisy is at play.   12

A sacrifice is governed by dark inertia
when it violates the norms—
empty of faith, omitting the ritual offering
of food and chants and gifts.   13

Honoring gods, priests,
teachers, and wise men, being pure,
honest, celibate, and nonviolent
is called bodily penance.   14

Speaking truth without offense,
giving comfort,
and reciting sacred lore
is called verbal penance.   15

Mental serenity, kindness,
silence, self-restraint,
and purity of being
is called mental penance.   16

This threefold penance
is lucid when men of discipline
perform it with deep faith,
without craving for reward.   17

Wavering and unstable,
performed with hypocrisy,
to gain respect, honor, and worship,
that penance is called passionate.   18

Performed with deluded perception,
self-mortification,
or sadism,
such penance has dark inertia.   19

Given in due time and place
to a fit recipient
who can give no advantage,
charity is remembered as lucid.   20

But charity given reluctantly,
to secure some service in return
or to gain a future reward,
is remembered as passionate.   21

Charity given out of place and time
to an unfit recipient,
ungraciously and with contempt,
is remembered for its dark inertia.   22

OM TAT SAT: "That Is the Real"—
this is the triple symbol of the infinite spirit
that gave a primordial sanctity
to priests, sacred lore, and sacrifice.   23

OM—knowers of the infinite spirit
chant it as they perform
acts of sacrifice, charity, and penance
prescribed by tradition.   24

TAT—men who crave freedom
utter it as they perform
acts of sacrifice, charity, and penance,
without concern for reward.   25

SAT—it means what is real
and what is good, Arjuna;
the word *SAT* is also used
when an action merits praise.   26

SAT is steadfastness in sacrifice,
in penance, in charity;
any action of this order
is denoted by *SAT*.   27

But oblation, charity,
and penance offered without faith
are called *ASAT,* for they have no reality
here or in the world after death.   28

The Eighteenth Teaching

THE WONDROUS DIALOGUE CONCLUDES

Arjuna

Krishna, I want to know
the real essence
of both renunciation
and relinquishment.   1

Lord Krishna

Giving up actions based on desire,
the poets know as "renunciation";
relinquishing all fruit of action,
learned men call "relinquishment."   2

Some wise men say all action
is flawed and must be relinquished;
others say action in sacrifice, charity,
and penance must not be relinquished.   3

Arjuna, hear my decision
about relinquishment;
it is rightly declared
to be of three kinds.   4

Action in sacrifice, charity,
and penance is to be performed,
not relinquished—for wise men,
they are acts of sanctity.   5

But even these actions
should be done by relinquishing to me
attachment and the fruit of action—
this is my decisive idea.   6

Renunciation of prescribed action
is inappropriate;
relinquished in delusion,
it becomes a way of dark inertia.   7

When one passionately relinquishes
difficult action from fear
of bodily harm, he cannot win
the fruit of relinquishment.   8

But if one performs prescribed action
because it must be done,
relinquishing attachment and the fruit,
his relinquishment is a lucid act.   9

He does not disdain unskilled action
nor cling to skilled action;
in his lucidity the relinquisher
is wise and his doubts are cut away.   10

A man burdened by his body
cannot completely relinquish actions,
but a relinquisher is defined
as one who can relinquish the fruits.   11

The fruit of action haunts men
in death if they fail to relinquish
all forms, unwanted, wanted, and mixed—
but not if men renounce them.   12

Arjuna, learn from me
the five causes
for the success of all actions
as explained in philosophical analysis.   13

They are the material basis,
the agent, the different instruments,
various kinds of behavior,
and finally fate, the fifth.   14

Whatever action one initiates
through body, speech, and mind,
be it proper or perverse,
these five causes are present.   15

This being so, when a man
of poor understanding and misjudgment
sees himself as the only agent,
he cannot be said to see.   16

When one is free of individuality
and his understanding is untainted,
even if he kills these people,
he does not kill and is not bound.   17

Knowledge, its object, and its subject
are the triple stimulus of action;
instrument, act, and agent
are the constituents of action.   18

Knowledge, action, agent are threefold,
differentiated by qualities of nature;
hear how this has been explained
in the philosophical analysis of qualities.   19

Know that through lucid knowledge
one sees in all creatures
a single, unchanging existence,
undivided within its divisions.   20

Know passionate knowledge
as that which regards
various distinct existences
separately in all creatures.   21

But knowledge that clings
to a single thing as if it were the whole,
limited, lacking a sense of reality,
is known for its dark inertia.   22

Action known for its lucidity
is necessary, free of attachment,
performed without attraction or hatred
by one who seeks no fruit.   23

Action called passionate
is performed with great effort
by an individualist
who seeks to satisfy his desires.   24

Action defined by dark inertia
is undertaken in delusion,
without concern for consequences,
for death or violence, or for manhood.   25

An agent called pure
has no attachment or individualism,
is resolute and energetic,
unchanged in failure and success.   26

An agent said to be passionate
is anxious to gain the fruit of action,
greedy, essentially violent, impure,
subject to excitement and grief.   27

An agent defined by dark inertia
is undisciplined, vulgar, stubborn,
fraudulent, dishonest, lazy,
depressed, and slow to act.   28

Listen as I tell you without reserve
about understanding and resolve,
each in three aspects,
according to the qualities of nature.   29

In one who knows activity and rest,
acts of right and wrong,
bravery and fear, bondage and freedom,
understanding is lucid.   30

When one fails to discern
sacred duty from chaos,
right acts from wrong,
understanding is passionate.   31

When it thinks in perverse ways,
is covered in darkness,
imagining chaos to be sacred duty,
understanding is darkly inert.   32

When it sustains acts
of mind, breath, and senses
through discipline without wavering,
resolve is lucid.   33

When it sustains with attachment
duty, desire, and wealth,
craving their fruits,
resolve is passionate.   34

When a fool cannot escape
dreaming, fear, grief,
depression, and intoxication,
courage is darkly inert.   35

Arjuna, now hear about joy,
the three ways of finding delight
through practice
that brings an end to suffering.   36

The joy of lucidity
at first seems like poison
but is in the end like ambrosia,
from the calm of self-understanding.   37

The joy that is passionate
at first seems like ambrosia
when senses encounter sense objects,
but in the end it is like poison.   38

The joy arising from sleep,
laziness, and negligence,
self-deluding from beginning to end,
is said to be darkly inert.   39

There is no being on earth
or among the gods in heaven
free from the triad of qualities
that are born of nature.   40

The actions of priests, warriors,
commoners, and servants
are apportioned by qualities
born of their intrinsic being.   41

Tranquility, control, penance,
purity, patience and honesty,
knowledge, judgment, and piety
are intrinsic to the action of a priest.   42

Heroism, fiery energy, resolve,
skill, refusal to retreat in battle,
charity, and majesty in conduct
are intrinsic to the action of a warrior.   43

Farming, herding cattle, and commerce
are intrinsic to the action of a commoner;
action that is essentially service
is intrinsic to the servant.   44

Each one achieves success
by focusing on his own action;
hear how one finds success
by focusing on his own action.   45

By his own action a man finds success,
worshipping the source
of all creatures' activity,
the presence pervading all that is.   46

Better to do one's own duty imperfectly
than to do another man's well;
doing action intrinsic to his being,
a man avoids guilt.   47

Arjuna, a man should not relinquish
action he is born to, even if it is flawed;
all undertakings are marred by a flaw,
as fire is obscured by smoke.   48

His understanding everywhere detached,
the self mastered, longing gone,
one finds through renunciation
the supreme success beyond action.   49

Understand in summary from me
how when he achieves success
one attains the infinite spirit,
the highest state of knowledge.   50

Armed with his purified understanding,
subduing the self with resolve,
relinquishing sensuous objects,
avoiding attraction and hatred;   51

Observing solitude, barely eating,
restraining speech, body, and mind;
practicing discipline in meditation,
cultivating dispassion;   52

Freeing himself from individuality, force,
pride, desire, anger, acquisitiveness;
unpossessive, tranquil,
he is at one with the infinite spirit.   53

Being at one with the infinite spirit,
serene in himself, he does not grieve or crave;
impartial toward all creatures,
he achieves supreme devotion to me.   54

Through devotion he discerns me,
just who and how vast I really am;
and knowing me in reality,
he enters into my presence.   55

Always performing all actions,
taking refuge in me,
he attains through my grace
the eternal place beyond change.   56

Through reason, renounce all works
in me, focus on me;
relying on the discipline of understanding,
always keep me in your thought.   57

If I am in your thought, by my grace
you will transcend all dangers;
but if you are deafened
by individuality, you will be lost.   58

Your resolve is futile
if a sense of individuality
makes you think, "I shall not fight"—
nature will compel you to.   59

You are bound by your own action,
intrinsic to your being, Arjuna;
even against your will you must do
what delusion now makes you refuse.   60

Arjuna, the lord resides
in the heart of all creatures,
making them reel magically,
as if a machine moved them.   61

With your whole being, Arjuna,
take refuge in him alone—
from his grace you will attain
the eternal place that is peace.   62

This knowledge I have taught
is more arcane than any mystery—
consider it completely,
then act as you choose.   63

Listen to my profound words,
the deepest mystery of all,
for you are precious to me
and I tell you for your good.   64

Keep your mind on me,
be my devotee, sacrificing, bow to me—
you will come to me, I promise,
for you are dear to me.   65

Relinquishing all sacred duties to me,
make me your only refuge;
do not grieve,
for I shall free you from all evils.   66

You must not speak of this
to one who is without penance and devotion,
or who does not wish to hear,
or who finds fault with me.   67

When he shares this deepest mystery
with others devoted to me,
giving me his total devotion,
a man will come to me without doubt.   68

No mortal can perform
service for me that I value more,
and no other man on earth
will be more dear to me than he is.   69

I judge the man who studies
our dialogue on sacred duty
to offer me sacrifice
through sacrifice in knowledge.   70

If he listens in faith,
finding no fault, a man is free
and will attain the cherished worlds
of those who act in virtue.   71

Arjuna, have you listened
with your full powers of reason?
Has the delusion of ignorance
now been destroyed?   72

Arjuna

Krishna, my delusion is destroyed,
and by your grace I have regained memory;
I stand here, my doubt dispelled,
ready to act on your words.   73

Sanjaya

As I heard this wondrous dialogue
between Krishna and Arjuna,
the man of great soul,
the hair bristled on my flesh.   74

By grace of the epic poet Vyasa, I heard
the mystery of supreme discipline
recounted by Krishna himself,
the lord of discipline incarnate.   75

O King, when I keep remembering
this wondrous and holy dialogue
between Krishna and Arjuna,
I rejoice again and again.   76

In my memory I recall again
and again Krishna's wondrous form—
great is my amazement, King;
I rejoice again and again.   77

Where Krishna is lord of discipline
and Arjuna is the archer,
there do fortune, victory, abundance,
and morality exist, so I think.   78

AFTERWORD

Why Did Henry David Thoreau Take the Bhagavad-Gita *to Walden Pond?*

Among the many works of Asian literature that were studied in Concord, Massachusetts, in the mid-nineteenth century, none was more influential than the *Bhagavad-Gita*. Ralph Waldo Emerson wrote of it in his journal of 1845:

> I owed—my friend and I owed—a magnificent day to the *Bhagavat Geeta*. It was the first of books; it was as if an empire spoke to us, nothing small or unworthy, but large, serene, consistent, the voice of an old intelligence which in another age and climate had pondered and thus disposed of the same questions which exercise us.

References to the *Gita* are found throughout Emerson's journals and letters, where he frequently quotes from the 1785 translation of Charles Wilkins's, on which Thoreau's readings are also based. Emerson is chiefly interested in Krishna's teaching that works must be done without thought of reward and that a person may have a tranquil mind even in activity.

The fascination that the *Gita* held for Thoreau and Emerson is, of course, only one component of their work, but it is the component most likely to perplex students of Western thought. By attempting to penetrate the levels at which they deliberately incorporated the "exotic" concepts and images of Hindu literature into their life and work, one can gain fresh insights into their thought and the thought of the ancient Indian sages with whom they felt such strong affinities. The Asian texts that Thoreau and Emerson were reading presented ideas that strengthened their critique of eighteenth-century rationalism and nineteenth-century materialism, while providing a new set of images, myths, and concepts expressive of man's spiritual energy.

In *Walden*, the book named for the pond in Concord where Thoreau lived from 1845 to 1847, he expresses his profound response to the *Gita* as he observes ice being cut from Walden Pond to be transported to India by New England merchants:

> Thus it appears that the sweltering inhabitants of Charleston and New Orleans, of Madras and Bombay and Calcutta, drink at my well. In the morning I bathe my intellect in the stupendous and cosmogonal philosophy of the Bhagvat Geeta, since whose composition years of the gods have elapsed, and in comparison with which our modern world and its literature seem puny and trivial; and I doubt if that philosophy is not to be referred to a previous state of existence, so remote is its sublimity from our conceptions. I lay down my book and go to my well for water, and lo! there I meet the servant of the Bramin, priest of Brahma and Vishnu and Indra, who still sits in his temple on the Ganges reading the Vedas, or dwells at the root of a tree with his crust and water jug. I meet his servant come to draw water for his master, and our buckets as it were grate together in the same well. The pure Walden water is mingled with the sacred water of the Ganges.

Thoreau offers a commentary on the *Gita* in his first major work, *A Week on the Concord and Merrimack Rivers*. In the chapter "Monday," he says:

> The wisest conservatism is that of the Hindoos. "Immemorial custom is transcendent law," says Menu. That is, it was the custom of the gods before men used it. The fault of our New England custom is that it is memorial. What is morality but immemorial custom? Conscience is the chief of conservatives. "Perform the settled functions," says Kreeshna in the Bhagvat Geeta, "action is preferable to inaction. The journey of thy mortal frame may not succeed from inaction."—"A

man's own calling with all its faults, ought not to be forsaken. Every undertaking is involved in its faults as the fire in its smoke."—"The man who is acquainted with the whole, should ·not drive those from their works who are slow of comprehension, and less experienced than himself."—"Wherefore, O Arjoon, resolve to fight,"—is the advice of the God to the irresolute soldier who fears to slay his best friends. It is a sublime conservatism; as wide as the world, and as unwearied as time; preserving the universe with Asiatic anxiety, in that state in which it appeared to their minds. . . .

> The end is an immense consolation, eternal absorption in Brahma.

Thoreau is clearly impressed by Krishna's critique of inaction, but he is reluctant to accept the morality of Krishna's argument, despite its being what he calls the "wisest conservatism." On one level the *Gita* does appear to justify violence. Arjuna is urged by Krishna to go to war against his kinsmen-enemies because war is his duty as a warrior and because death is inevitable. But the *Gita* is not a justification of war, nor does it propound a war-making mystique, as men of peace such as Mahatma Gandhi and the Trappist monk Thomas Merton knew when they read it. Merton argues that point with clarity in his essay "The Significance of the *Bhagavad Gita*":

> Arjuna has an instinctive repugnance for war, and that is the chief reason why war is chosen as the example of the most repellent kind of duty. The *Gita* is saying that even in what appears to be the most "unspiritual," one can act with pure intentions and thus be guided by Krishna consciousness. This consciousness itself will impose the most strict limitations on one's own use of violence because that use will not be directed by one's own selfish interests, still less by cruelty, sadism, and blood-lust.

Another sympathetic modern reader of the *Gita*, E. M. Forster, writing about it in the *Cambridge Review* in

1920, during the period he was working on *A Passage to India*, deals with the issues of action and war in similar terms. Forster points to three of Krishna's reasons why Arjuna must fight. The first assumes that death is negligible; the second that duty is ᵴacred. Krishna's third reason is the most profound: it taɪᵌs up the problem of renunciation and attempts to harmonize the needs of life with eternal truth. Forster interprets it this way:

> The saint may renounce action, but the soldier, the citizen, the practical man generally—they should renounce, not action, but its fruits. It is wrong for them to be idle; it is equally wrong to desire a reward for industry. It is wrong to shirk destroying civilization and one's kindred and friends, equally wrong to hope for dominion afterwards. When all such hopes and desires are dead fear dies also, and freed from all attachments the "dweller in the body" will remain calm while the body performs its daily duty, and will be unstained by sin, as is the lotus leaf by the water of the tank. It will attain to the eternal peace that is offered to the practical man as well as to the devotee. It will have abjured the wages of action, which are spiritual death, and gained in their place a vision of the Divine.

For Thoreau, with his interest in the interpenetration of places and states of mind, the imagery of Arjuna's heroic struggle to know himself on the spiritual battlefield of Kuru gave the *Gita* personal significance. There are clues to this in *A Week on the Concord and Merrimack Rivers*, where he discusses the *Gita* in terms of what it means to be a hero. If one reads the parable of the artist of Kouroo in the conclusion of *Walden* from this perspective, it seems to be Thoreau's translation of Krishna's teaching into artistic terms. The artist's skilled dedication to the perfect work is what Krishna means by spiritual discipline. It is in a state of total involvement that one finds liberation from time.

There was an artist in the city of Kouroo who was disposed to strive after perfection. One day it came into his mind to make a staff. Having considered that in an imperfect work time is an ingredient, but into a perfect work time does not enter, he said to himself, It shall be perfect in all respects, though I should do nothing else in my life. He proceeded instantly to the forest for wood, being resolved that it should not be made of unsuitable material; and as he searched for and rejected stick after stick, his friends gradually deserted him, for they grew old in their works and died, but he grew not older by a moment. His singleness of purpose and resolution, and his elevated piety, endowed him, without his knowledge, with perennial youth. As he made no compromise with Time, Time kept out of his way, and only sighed at a distance because he could not overcome him. Before he had found a stock in all respects suitable the city of Kouroo was a hoary ruin, and he sat on one of its mounds to peel the stick. Before he had given it the proper shape the dynasty of the Candahars was at an end, and with the point of the stick he wrote the name of the last of that race in the sand, and then resumed his work. By the time he had smoothed and polished the staff Kalpa was no longer the pole-star; and ere he had put on the ferule and the head adorned with precious stones, Brahma had awoke and slumbered many times. But why do I stay to mention these things? When the finishing stroke was put to his work, it suddenly expanded before the eyes of the astonished artist into the fairest of all creations of Brahma. He had made a new system in making a staff, a world with full and fair proportions; in which, though the old cities and dynasties had passed away, fairer and more glorious ones had taken their places. And now he saw by the heap of shavings still fresh at his feet, that, for him and his work, the former lapse of time had been an illusion, and that no more time had elapsed than is required for a single scintillation from the brain of Brahma to fall on and inflame the tinder of a mortal brain. The material was pure, and his art was pure; how could the result be other than wonderful?

Thoreau was moved by his own observation that the mass of his fellow men led "lives of quiet desperation."

He sought to discover freedom from that desperation by refusing to be led by the senses and passions, by living deliberately, by simplifying his life in order to internalize the solitude of a place in nature. He lived at Walden for two years and two months, during which time he confined his desires and his actions in such a way that he strove to overcome the limitations of time and absorb himself in nature.

Nature was for him the ground of religious life. In the section of *Walden* entitled "Higher Laws" he says:

Every man is the builder of a temple, called his body, to the god he worships, after a style purely his own, nor can he get off by hammering marble instead. We are all sculptors and painters, and our material is our own flesh and blood and bones. Any nobleness begins at once to refine a man's features, any meanness or sensuality to imbrute them.

John Farmer sat at his door one September evening, after a hard day's work, his mind still running on his labor more or less. Having bathed he sat down to recreate his intellectual man. It was a rather cool evening, and some of his neighbors were apprehending a frost. He had not attended to the train of his thoughts long when he heard someone playing on a flute, and that sound harmonized with his mood. Still he thought of his work; but the burden of his thought was, that though this kept running in his head, and he found himself planning and contriving it against his will, yet it concerned him very little. It was no more than the scurf of his skin, which was constantly shuffled off. But the notes of the flute came home to his ears out of a different sphere from that he worked in, and suggested work for certain faculties which slumbered in him. They gently did away with the street, and the village, and the state in which he lived. A voice said to him,—Why do you stay here and live this mean moiling life, when a glorious existence is possible for you? Those same stars twinkle over other fields than these. — But how to come out of this condition and actually migrate thither? All that he could think of was to practice some new austerity, to let his mind descend into his body and redeem it, and treat himself with ever increasing respect.

The ascetic, mystical love of nature that brought Thoreau to Walden Pond gave him access to the central teaching of the *Gita*. He perceived the discipline of living in nature as a path leading toward self-knowledge and spiritual realization. He writes in his journal in 1841:

One may discover the root of a Hindoo religion in his own private history, when, in the silent intervals of the day or night, he does sometimes inflict on himself like austerities with stern satisfaction.

In *Walden* he emphatically states, "My purpose in going to Walden Pond was not to live cheaply nor to live dearly there but to transact some private business with the fewest obstacles." Walden was for Thoreau a spiritual retreat where he strove to deepen his understanding of his existence and through this understanding to gain release from the terrible bondage of life's compelling illusions. In Indian terms it was the retreat of a yogi who carefully practiced spiritual discipline. In a letter of 1849 to his friend H.G.O. Blake, he wrote about yoga and its private meaning for him:

"Free in this world as the birds in the air, disengaged from every kind of chains, those who practice the yoga gather in Brahma the certain fruits of their works.

Depend upon it that, rude and careless as I am, I would fain practice the yoga faithfully.

"The yogi, absorbed in contemplation, contributes in his degree to creation; he breathes a divine perfume, he hears wonderful things. Divine forms traverse him without tearing him, and united to the nature which is proper to him, he goes, he acts as animating original matter."

To some extent, and at rare intervals,
even I am a yogi.

KEY WORDS IN THE
Bhagavad-Gita

The structure of the *Gita* is characterized by the way in which central concepts are consistently repeated and reinterpreted, giving the text its own inner interpretive code. This process of explication is shaped by the form of the dialogue itself, in which Arjuna poses questions and seeks clarification of the key ideas in Krishna's doctrine. The responses to these questions present varying ways of transcending the limitations of phenomenal existence. Philosophical analysis, practical discipline, metaphysical knowledge, and devotion are not mutually exclusive methods, but aspects of a comprehensive approach to the human dilemma of living in a transient, chaotic world. In the *Gita*, in order to integrate the ideas of these different methods of inquiry, key words common to them take on special significance.

Given the highly concentrated vocabulary of the *Gita*, my notes on the English translations of these key words are offered as a way of understanding the core of the text. The interpretation of terms is based mainly on internal definitions within the *Gita* itself. The meanings of these terms in the wider Hindu tradition are referred to only where particularly relevant to the *Gita*. My understanding of individual words and passages has been influenced by the commentaries of Shankara and Ramanuja, as well as by several Western studies of the *Gita*.

For readers who want further guidance through detailed analysis of individual passages, I recommend several works that interpret the text with scholarly care.

The Bhagavad-Gita Translated and Interpreted, by Franklin Edgerton, 2 vols. (Cambridge: Harvard University Press, 1952).
Bhagavad-Gita: An Exegetical Commentary, by Robert N. Minor (Columbia, MO: South Asia Books, 1982).
Ramanuja on the Bhagavadgita, by J. A. B. van Buitenen (Delhi: Motilal Banarsidass, 1968).
*The Bhagavad-Gita: With Commentary Based on the Original

Sources, by R. C. Zaehner (London: Oxford University Press, 1969).

A good bibliographic survey on the *Gita* is available in the volume *Bhagavadgitanuvada: A Study in Transcultural Translation*, by W. M. Callewaert and S. Hemraj (Ranchi: Satya Bharati Publication, 1983).

A Note on Sanskrit Pronunciation

Commonly known Sanskrit words and proper names are anglicized in accordance with spellings in *Webster's Third New International Dictionary*. Sanskrit technical terms are rendered in italic script, with appropriate diacritical marks. Vowels, except *a*, which is pronounced as the *u* in *cut*, are given their full value, as in Italian. Most consonants are analogous to English, if the distinction between aspirated and nonaspirated consonants is observed. For example, the aspirated consonants *bh* and *ph* are not pronounced as in English *th*in and *ph*ial, but as in club*h*ouse and she*ph*erd (similarly, *kh, gh, ch, jh, th, dh*). Another distinctive feature of Sanskrit is the difference between the "cerebral" consonants *ṭ, ṭh, ḍ, ḍh, ṇ, ṣ* and the "dental" consonants *t, th, d, dh, n, s*. The dentals are formed with the tongue against the teeth, the cerebrals with the tongue flexed back along the palate. Also, the consonant *g* is pronounced as the *g* in *goat; c* as the *ch* in *church; ś* as the *s* in *sugar*, anglicized as *sh*.

In reading Sanskrit words, the accent may be placed on a heavy syllable: a syllable containing a long simple vowel (*ā, ī, ū*), a diphthong (*e, o, ai, au*), or a short vowel followed by more than one consonant.

ACTION *(karma)*—from the Sanskrit root *kṛ*, "to do," "to act." *Karma* refers to the force of one's actions in determining what one is and will be, to one's role in making one's own destiny. In theory *karma* is a store of good and bad actions accumulated over many lives, and it is this store of actions that binds one to phenomenal existence. Only when one acts without concern for the consequences, or fruits, of one's action can one escape the bondage of action. Krishna's teaching that action is inescapable is central to the entire *Gita*.

DELUSION *(moha)*—from the Sanskrit root *muh*, "to be confused" or "to lose consciousness." Delusion, which is linked in early Indian thought with passionate affection *(rāga)* and aversion *(dveṣa)*, blinds one to reality; perception of truth can be restored through knowledge and faith.

DESIRE *(kāma)*—sensuous love, emotional feeling of attachment. In ancient Indian thought it is recognized as the stimulus of action and personified as the god of erotic love. In the *Gita*, as in Buddhism, it is the source of attachment to the world and the great impediment to spiritual freedom. Krishna tells Arjuna, "Kill the enemy menacing you in the form of desire!" (3.43).

DEVOTION *(bhakti)*—from the Sanskrit root *bhaj*, "to share," from which is also derived the word *bhagavat*, "lord," referring to Lord Krishna as the object of devotion who shares in the life of his devotee. In the *Gita* devotion is a discipline *(bhaktiyoga)* involving the performance of disciplined action *(karmayoga)* without personal attachment and with dedication of the fruits to Krishna. This devotion enables one to engage actively in the world and still have spiritual freedom. Through devotion the self expands toward the infinite and the infinite is brought to a conceivable human scale.

DISCIPLINE *(yoga)*—from the Sanskrit root *yuj*, "to yoke." In the *Gita* it is the yoking of oneself to Krishna's divine purpose, the spiritual and physical discipline that integrates aspects of reality. It is defined as "equanimity" *(samatva, 2.48)* and "skill in actions" *(karma-kauśala, 2.50)*, "unbinding the bonds of suffering" *(duḥkhasaṁyogaviyoga, 6.23)*. It is directly related to knowledge of the discipline and power of Krishna (10.7), who is the lord of discipline *(yogeśvara)*. In the *Gita*, *yoga* also refers to the codified system of practical discipline called Yoga (in contrast to the system of philosophical analysis called Sankhya) and to each of the ways of reaching liberation, the most important of which are the discipline of action *(karmayoga)*, the discipline of knowledge *(jñānayoga)*, and the discipline of devotion *(bhaktiyoga)*. One who practices discipline is called a "man of discipline" *(yogī)*.

DUTY *(dharma)*—sacred duty, order, law; from the Sanskrit root *dhṛ*, "to sustain." A concept of complex significance in Indian culture, its basic meaning is "that which sustains," i.e., the moral order that sustains the individual, the society, and the cosmos. *Dharma* generally refers to religiously ordained duty; in the *Gita*, as in other Hindu texts, this means the rules of conduct appropriate to the various diverse groups in a hierarchically ordered society, articulated in terms of class, stage of life, and kinship structures. The general notion exists that if each unit or group in the manifold and complex universe performs its own function correctly, the whole (the individual, the society, and the cosmos) will be harmonious and ordered.

FAITH (*śraddhā*)—giving oneself up to dependency on Krishna, the object of devotion, who grants unwavering faith to his devotee (7.21) and so dispels his doubt.

FIELD (*kṣetra*)—the battlefield of Kuru, associated with the legendary king Kuru who performed penance there, identified in *BG* 1.1 as the field of sacred duty (*dharmakṣetra*). At *BG* 13.1 the field is said to denote the body, the locus of the self, who is called the field-knower (*kṣetrajña*). The field of battle in the *Gita* is thus the whole field of human experience, the realm of material nature in which the struggle for self-knowledge occurs.

FRUIT (*phala*)—the fruit, consequence, or reward of action (*karmaphala*). All action has inevitable consequences, which accumulate through succeeding rebirths. By relinquishing attachment and dedicating the fruit of action to Krishna, one can gain liberation (2.47, 51; 5.12; 18.6, 12).

GRACE (*prasāda*)—divine grace or favor, from the Sanskrit root *sad* with the prefix *pra*, "to become clear or calm." Through Krishna's grace Arjuna sees the cosmic totality and his delusion is dispelled.

INDIVIDUALITY (*ahaṁkāra*)—literally "I-maker," the ego, the subjective sense of individual identity. In its cosmogonic aspect in classical Sankhya philosophy, individuality is an evolute of nature, like insight, mind, and the senses. The idea is that the empirical world cannot emerge before an individual consciousness (*aham*) has evolved. Implicitly this means that liberation from empirical existence involves the negation of individuality.

INFINITE SPIRIT (*brahman*)—usually translated as the "Absolute." In Vedic literature it means "prayer," or the power of the ritual word. In Vedanta it comes to mean the ultimate reality underlying phenomenal existence; it is vast, unqualified, and imperishable. Both of these meanings are present in the *Gita*, where the macrocosmic infinite spirit (*brahman*) corresponds to the microcosmic self (*ātman*) within each individual. When the self has achieved identification with the infinite spirit, one is said to have found "the pure calm of infinity" (*brahmanirvāṇa*, a compounding of *brahman* with the Buddhist term for the cessation of suffering that is perfect calm *[nirvāṇa]*; 2.72, 5.24–26). In the *Gita* the infinite spirit is superseded by Lord Krishna, who says he is the very foundation of the infinite (*brahmaṇo hi pratiṣṭhā 'ham*, 14.27). *Brahman*, the infinite spirit, is etymologically related to Brahmā, the cosmic creator; they are differentiated in Sanskrit by gender, the infinite being neuter, the creator masculine.

JOY *(sukha)*—happiness, in contrast to suffering *(duḥkha)*; a duality toward which one must develop equanimity.

KNOWLEDGE *(jñāna)*—from the Sanskrit root *jñā*, "to know." The theme of section four of the *Gita*, it is paired with judgment *(vijñāna)* in the seventh section. The contrast between them is between nonconceptual, spiritual knowledge of transcendental reality and apperceptive, logical knowledge of the world.

LIBERATION *(mokṣa)*—freedom; from the Sanskrit root *muc*, "to release." In the *Gita* liberation from the bondage of worldly action is based on detachment and freedom within oneself.

MAGIC *(māyā)*—creative illusion, magic power, from the Sanskrit root *mā*, "to measure," "to form." Veiled in the magic of his discipline *(yogamāyāsamāvṛta*, 7.25), Krishna comes into being through his own divine magic (4.6), which can be creative or destructive for humans (7.14–15).

MAN, MAN'S SPIRIT *(puruṣa)*—a person's essential being; pure consciousness, in contrast to nature *(prakṛti)*, which is unconscious material potentiality. These two are the basic categories of Indian philosophical analysis *(sāṅkhya)*. Like the self *(ātman)*, man's spirit is the life principle whose reality is independent of everything that is compounded of the properties of nature and is thus detached from the activity of the world. It is the person behind the construct of understanding, individuality, mind, and senses, which are evolutes of nature and should not be confused with them—such delusion creates a mistaken identity of man's spirit with nature and binds him to the phenomenal world (3.27–29). Krishna is called "supreme among men," or "man's highest spirit" *(puruṣottama)*.

MEMORY *(smṛti)*—intuitive insight into the past that transcends personal experience. Not discursive recollection of past events, but the awakening of latent impressions left by prior perceptions; essential to the aesthetic experience of Krishna's revelation (18. 73, 76, 77).

MIND *(manas)*—the faculty of perception and cognition, by which objects of sense affect insight; distinct from the five senses, but like them an evolute of nature.

NATURE *(prakṛti)*—primal material nature in contrast to man's spirit *(puruṣa)*; also called the unmanifest *(avyakta)*, the potential out of which the manifest world evolves. Every aspect of the phenomenal world (all subjects, objects, and effects) is inherent in nature. Nature is made up of the three qualities *(triguṇa)* that constitute it; when they are in a state of equilibrium, there is no evolution and nature remains unmanifest. (See QUALITY OF NATURE.)

PEACE *(śānti)*—tranquility, the absence of desire, the concomitant of joy (2.66).

PENANCE *(tapas)*—austerity, ascetic practice; from the Sanskrit root *tap*, "to be hot." In Indian symbolism heat is both desire and ascetic penance. The forces derived from penance, such as charity and sacrifice, are traditional antidotes to desire.

PHILOSOPHY *(sāṅkhya)*—philosophical analysis, the system of theoretical philosophy that complements the practice of spiritual discipline in the *Gita*. The dominant epic philosophy of dualism distinguishes two ultimate constituents of existence: man's spirit and nature.

QUALITY OF NATURE *(guṇa)*—each of the three qualities that collectively constitute nature: lucidity *(sattva)*, passion *(rajas)*, and dark inertia *(tamas)*. Together they are the basis of every aspect of phenomenal existence. No single quality causes anything, but the nature of each individual depends on which quality prevails in it. The three strands of nature intertwine to make the rope that binds man's spirit to the world (14.5–20).

REASON *(cetas)*—the reasoning faculty, the power of comprehending or inferring; from the Sanskrit root *cit*, "to comprehend." Though often translated "mind," in the *Gita* it is distinct from mind *(manas)*, which is an evolute of nature.

RELINQUISHMENT *(tyāga)*—from the Sanskrit root *tyaj*, "to relinquish" or "to abandon." It is defined in the *Gita* as "relinquishing all fruit of action" *(sarvakarmaphalatyāga,* 18.2) in contrast with renunciation, though the two terms are sometimes conflated. Relinquishment means that action is to be performed, but without concern for the fruit.

RENUNCIATION *(sannyāsa)*—from the Sanskrit root *as* with the prefixes *sam* and *ni,* "to cast down." It is variously defined in the *Gita,* in terms of surrendering all actions to Krishna (3.30), being without hate and desire (5.3), and giving up actions based on desire (18.2). Disciplined action and relinquishment are spiritually more effective than renunciation.

SACRED LORE *(veda)*—the body of ancient hymns and ancillary liturgical texts preserved in an oral tradition by the priestly class. The "threefold sacred lore" refers to the three collections of hymns, the oldest and most sacred being the *Rig Veda.*

SACRIFICE *(yajña)*—sacrificial rite. In the ancient Vedic fire cult the purpose of sacrifice was to ensure the well-being of the individual and the community by maintaining a ritual relation to the gods. In the *Gita* (3.9–16; 4.23–33), the orthodox idea of sacrifice is transformed to mean that all action is to be performed as sacrifice.

SELF *(ātman)*—also translated "soul" or "spirit," it is the innermost reality of a person, the animate, spiritual principle of life, not to be confused with gross individuality *(ahamkāra).* "The self is its own friend and its own worst foe," says Krishna (6.5). A person whose self is great is called a "great soul" *(mahātma),* the translation "great spirit" is used for Krishna.

TIME *(kāla)*—a word that also means "death." In Indian thought time is without beginning, endless, all-pervading. In the *Gita,* Krishna identifies himself as indestructible time that destroys the worlds (10.30, 33; 11.32).

UNDERSTANDING *(buddhi)*—the collective rational powers, including intuitive intelligence; the intellectual capacity to form reasoned judgments; in contrast to mind, which is the discursive intellect. In the early Indian system of philosophical analysis, both, along with the sense faculties, are classed as evolutes of nature and are transcended by man's spirit. According to a simile in the *Katha Upanishad* (1.3.3–4), the human body is like a chariot whose steeds are the senses, mind the reins, and understanding the charioteer, and the self the owner of the chariot. Understanding thus controls the senses through the mind and can guide a human being toward his self-fulfillment.

ABOUT THE TRANSLATOR

BARBARA STOLER MILLER is a translator of Sanskrit literature and interpreter of Asian cultures. She has traveled widely throughout Asia and lived in India to study Sanskrit, as well as Indian music and art. Her best-known book is *Love Song of the Dark Lord*, a verse translation and study of the medieval Indian religious erotic poem *Gitagovinda*. Among the many other works of poetry and drama she has edited and translated are *The Hermit and the Love-Thief: Sanskrit Poems of Bhartrihari and Bilhana* and *Theater of Memory: The Plays of Kalidasa*. Dr. Miller has also edited *Exploring India's Sacred Art: Selected Writings of Stella Kramrisch* and *Songs for the Bride: Wedding Rites of Rural India* by the late W. G. Archer and translated a volume of Spanish poetry, *Sombraventadora/Shadowinnower* by Agueda Pizarro de Rayo. Currently she is editing a volume of essays entitled "Patronage in Indian Culture: Art, Religion, and Politics" and working on a translation of the life of the Buddha, based on the first century A.D. poem *Buddhacarita*.

Dr. Miller studied philosophy as an undergraduate at Barnard College and holds a doctorate in Sanskrit and Indic Studies from the University of Pennsylvania. She has been a Guggenheim Fellow and has received grants from the Ford Foundation, the Smithsonian Institution, the National Endowment for the Humanities, and the American Council of Learned Societies. In 1979 she received the Award in Higher Education from the National Council of Women.

Chairman of the Department of Oriental Studies at Barnard College, Columbia University, where she has taught since 1968, Dr. Miller also codirects the Barnard humanities program and has lectured extensively at universities in North America, Europe, Asia, and Australia.

Bantam Classics bring you the world's greatest literature—books that have stood the test of time—at specially low prices. These beautifully designed books will be proud additions to your bookshelf. You'll want all these time-tested classics for your own reading pleasure.

☐ 21109 BEOWULF AND OTHER OLD $1.95
          ENGLISH POEMS
☐ 21082 CANTERBURY TALES, $2.95
          Geoffrey Chaucer
☐ 21179 THE PRINCE, Niccolo Machiavelli $1.75
☐ 21076 COMPLETE PLAYS, Sophocles $2.95
☐ 21169 THREE COMEDIES, Plautus $3.95
☐ 21041 THE AENEID, Virgil $2.95
☐ 21182 FAUST, Johann W. von Goethe $3.50
☐ 21166 CANDIDE, Voltaire $2.25
☐ 21164 COMPLETE PLAYS, Aristophanes $3.50
☐ 21219 TEN PLAYS, Euripides $3.50
☐ 21151 GREEK DRAMA, Hadas, ed. $3.50

Dante: THE DIVINE COMEDY

☐ 21069 INFERNO $2.50
☐ 21133 PURGATORIO $3.50
☐ 21204 PARADISO $4.95

Look for them at your bookstore or use this handy coupon: